The Literature of Cinema

ADVISORY EDITOR: **MARTIN S. DWORKIN**
INSTITUTE OF PHILOSOPHY AND POLITICS OF EDUCATION
TEACHER'S COLLEGE, COLUMBIA UNIVERSITY

THE LITERATURE OF CINEMA presents a comprehensive selection from the multitude of writings about cinema, rediscovering materials on its origins, history, theoretical principles and techniques, aesthetics, economics, and effects on societies and individuals. Included are works of inherent, lasting merit and others of primarily historical significance. These provide essential resources for serious study and critical enjoyment of the "magic shadows" that became one of the decisive cultural forces of modern times.

Movies, Delinquency, and Crime

Herbert Blumer and Philip M. Hauser

ARNO PRESS & THE NEW YORK TIMES

New York • 1970

109/26

Reprint Edition 1970 by Arno Press Inc.
Reprinted from a copy in The Museum of Modern Art Library
Library of Congress Catalog Card Number: 70-124024
ISBN 0-405-01641-7
ISBN for complete set: 0-405-01600-X
Manufactured in the United States of America

MOVIES, DELINQUENCY, AND CRIME

MOTION PICTURES AND YOUTH

THE PAYNE FUND STUDIES

W. W. Charters, Chairman

Motion Pictures and Youth: A Summary, by W. W. Charters, Director, Bureau of Educational Research, Ohio State University.

Combined with

Getting Ideas from the Movies, by P. W. Holaday, Indianapolis Public Schools, and George D. Stoddard, Director, Iowa Child Welfare Research Station.

Motion Pictures and the Social Attitudes of Children, by Ruth C. Peterson and L. L. Thurstone, Department of Psychology, University of Chicago.

Combined with

The Social Conduct and Attitudes of Movie Fans, by Frank K. Shuttleworth and Mark A. May, Institute of Human Relations, Yale University.

The Emotional Responses of Children to the Motion Picture Situation, by W. S. Dysinger and Christian A. Ruckmick, Department of Psychology, State University of Iowa.

Combined with

Motion Pictures and Standards of Morality, by Charles C. Peters, Professor of Education, Pennsylvania State College.

Children's Sleep, by Samuel Renshaw, Vernon L. Miller, and Dorothy Marquis, Department of Psychology, Ohio State University.

Movies and Conduct, by Herbert Blumer, Department of Sociology, University of Chicago.

The Content of Motion Pictures, by Edgar Dale, Research Associate, Bureau of Educational Research, Ohio State University.

Combined with

Children's Attendance at Motion Pictures, by Edgar Dale.

Movies, Delinquency, and Crime, by Herbert Blumer and Philip M. Hauser, Department of Sociology, University of Chicago.

Boys, Movies, and City Streets, by Paul G. Cressey and Frederick M. Thrasher, New York University.

How to Appreciate Motion Pictures, by Edgar Dale, Research Associate, Bureau of Educational Research, Ohio State University.

MOVIES, DELINQUENCY, AND CRIME

❖

HERBERT BLUMER
ASSOCIATE PROFESSOR OF SOCIOLOGY
UNIVERSITY OF CHICAGO

PHILIP M. HAUSER
INSTRUCTOR IN SOCIOLOGY
UNIVERSITY OF CHICAGO

NEW YORK
THE MACMILLAN COMPANY
1933

THIS SERIES OF TWELVE STUDIES OF THE
INFLUENCE OF MOTION PICTURES UPON
CHILDREN AND YOUTH HAS BEEN MADE BY
THE COMMITTEE ON EDUCATIONAL RE-
SEARCH OF THE PAYNE FUND AT THE RE-
QUEST OF THE NATIONAL COMMITTEE FOR
THE STUDY OF SOCIAL VALUES IN MOTION
PICTURES, NOW THE MOTION PICTURE RE-
SEARCH COUNCIL, 366 MADISON AVENUE,
NEW YORK CITY. THE STUDIES WERE DE-
SIGNED TO SECURE AUTHORITATIVE AND
IMPERSONAL DATA WHICH WOULD MAKE
POSSIBLE A MORE COMPLETE EVALUATION
OF MOTION PICTURES AND THEIR SOCIAL
POTENTIALITIES

CHAIRMAN'S PREFACE

MOTION PICTURES are not understood by the present generation of adults. They are new; they make an enormous appeal to children; and they present ideas and situations which parents may not like. Consequently when parents think of the welfare of their children who are exposed to these compelling situations, they wonder about the effect of the pictures upon the ideals and behavior of the children. Do the pictures really influence children in any direction? Are their conduct, ideals, and attitudes affected by the movies? Are the scenes which are objectionable to adults understood by children, or at least by very young children? Do children eventually become sophisticated and grow superior to pictures? Are the emotions of children harmfully excited? In short, just what effect do motion pictures have upon children of different ages?

Each individual has his answer to these questions. He knows of this or that incident in his own experience, and upon these he bases his conclusions. Consequently opinions differ widely. No one in this country up to the present time has known in any general and impersonal manner just what effect motion pictures have upon children. Meanwhile children clamor to attend the movies as often as they are allowed to go. Moving pictures make a profound appeal to children of all ages. In such a situation it is obvious that a comprehensive study of the influence of motion pictures upon children and youth is appropriate.

To measure these influences the investigators who cooperated to make this series of studies analyzed the problem to discover the most significant questions involved. They set up individual studies to ascertain the answer to the questions and to provide a composite answer to the central question of the nature and extent of these influences. In using this technique the answers must inevitably be sketches without all the details filled in; but when the details are added the picture will not be changed in any essential manner. Parents, educators, and physicians will have little difficulty in fitting concrete details of their own into the outlines which these studies supply.

Specifically, the studies were designed to form a series to answer the following questions: What sorts of scenes do the children of America see when they attend the theaters? How do the mores depicted in these scenes compare with those of the community? How often do children attend? How much of what they see do they remember? What effect does what they witness have upon their ideals and attitudes? Upon their sleep and health? Upon their emotions? Do motion pictures directly or indirectly affect the conduct of children? Are they related to delinquency and crime, and, finally, how can we teach children to discriminate between movies that are artistically and morally good and bad?

The history of the investigations is brief. In 1928 William H. Short, Executive Director of the Motion Picture Research Council, invited a group of university psychologists, sociologists, and educators to meet with the members of the Council to confer about the possibility of discovering just what effect motion pictures have upon children, a subject, as has been indicated, upon which many conflicting opinions and few substantial facts were in existence. The university men proposed a program of study. When Mr. Short appealed to The Payne Fund for a grant to support such an investigation, he found the foundation receptive because of its well-known interest in motion pictures as one of the major influences in the lives of modern youth. When the appropriation had been made the investigators organized themselves into a Committee on Educational Research of The Payne Fund with the following membership: L. L. Thurstone, Frank N. Freeman, R. E. Park, Herbert Blumer, Philip M. Hauser of the University of Chicago; George D. Stoddard, Christian A. Ruckmick, P. W. Holaday, and Wendell Dysinger of the University of Iowa; Mark A. May and Frank K. Shuttleworth of Yale University; Frederick M. Thrasher and Paul G. Cressey of New York University; Charles C. Peters of Pennsylvania State College; Ben D. Wood of Columbia University; and Samuel Renshaw, Edgar Dale, and W. W. Charters of Ohio State University. The investigations have extended through four years, 1929–1932 inclusive.

The committee's work is an illustration of an interesting technique for studying any social problem. The distinctive characteristic of this technique is to analyze a complex social problem into a series of subordinate problems, to select competent investigators to work upon each of the subordinate projects and to integrate the findings of all the investigators as a solution of the initial problem. Such a program yields a skeleton framework, which, while somewhat lacking in detail, is substantially correct if the contributing investigations have been validly conducted. To provide this framework or outline is the task of research. To fill in the detail and to provide the interpretations are the natural and easy tasks of those who use the data.

W. W. C.

Ohio State University
June, 1933

AUTHORS' PREFACE

IT IS a common practice to review the findings of a study in the preface. In this volume the summary and conclusions are presented in the final chapter.

The writers wish to acknowledge indebtedness to Dr. Paul L. Schroeder, State Criminologist and Director of the Institute for Juvenile Research, Mr. John.C. Weigel, Administrator of the Institute for Juvenile Research, and Mr. Clifford R. Shaw, Head Research Sociologist of the Institute for Juvenile Research, Chicago, Illinois. Successful entrée to the institutions in which many of our materials were secured was due, in no small measure, to their courtesy and coöperation. Appreciation is also due to Professor Edwin H. Sutherland of the University of Chicago, who on a number of occasions advised us in the construction of our schedule and guidance sheet forms. The coöperation of Mr. William B. Cox, Secretary of the National Society of Penal Information, in securing questionnaire responses from the directors of penitentiaries and reformatories was an especially valuable contribution to our work.

We wish also to acknowledge the assistance given in the collection of materials by Messrs. Maurice E. Moore and Jerome H. Sampson of the Institute for Juvenile Research, Miss Haseltine Byrd, Miss Cerna J. Sampson, Mr. Marquis Alderman, and Mr. Fred Hackney.

It is important to acknowledge our debt to the contributors whose materials have made possible this study. We wish to thank the heads of penal and correctional institutions who filled out and returned to us the lengthy schedule submitted to them; the grade-school children who answered questionnaires; the high-school boys and girls who patiently wrote their motion-picture autobiographies; and finally the inmates and ex-convicts who in a fine spirit of coöperation filled out questionnaires and wrote their life histories sometimes at considerable pains.

In compliance with editorial suggestions the names of motion pictures and actors have been omitted from many of the autobiographical excerpts given in the text. These deletions do not affect the central purpose of showing the relation of motion pictures to the problems dealt with in this volume.

H. B.
P. M. H.

Chicago, Illinois
January, 1933

TABLE OF CONTENTS

xi

MOVIES, DELINQUENCY, AND CRIME

CHAPTER I

PROBLEM AND PROCEDURE

MANY people believe that current commercial motion pictures are responsible in considerable measure for present-day crime and delinquency. Official censorship, state and municipal, as well as the denunciation by some groups of the showing of crime pictures are expressions of this belief. Many of these people decry the production of "crime" or "gangster" pictures, as fraught with dangerous possibilities of disposing youth to crime.

Opposed to this belief is the assertion of many people, particularly of the partisans of the movies, that motion pictures in general and crime pictures in particular do not dispose to crime; that quite the contrary is true, for by stressing the inevitable punishment of the criminal, motion pictures discourage crime and incidentally deter many who have criminal tendencies.

This disagreement in belief has set the problem of the present study—it is indicative of the absence of adequate information on the effects of motion pictures. Specifically the object of the investigation is to consider (1) the rôle of motion pictures in the lives of delinquents and criminals of both sexes; (2) the effects on the inmates of motion pictures shown at correctional schools, reformatories, and penitentiaries; and (3) some effects of crime pictures on non-delinquent boys and girls.

To study these three problems adequately and conclusively would require a treatment much more extensive and diversified than it has been possible to undertake in the present inquiry. We have sought to extend our investigation as far as could be done but considerations of time, finances, and facilities of research necessarily limit our study to a form of exploration.

In seeking to throw light on these problems we have depended mainly on personal accounts by individuals of their own experiences. More sophisticated and refined techniques of research, while of great value for certain problems, were not suited, in the opinion of the authors, for the exploratory work which our study required. We have assumed that personal accounts of experience secured under satisfactory conditions and interpreted with caution would be most serviceable in providing requisite information.

To this end we have collected a number of autobiographical accounts dealing with motion-picture experiences. From the earliest groups of such documents items of recurrent experience were taken and combined into a guidance sheet to assist subsequent informants in writing their documents.[1] The guidance sheet aided the writer to focus his attention on that sector of his experiences in which we were interested, and thereby give a full account without appreciable loss of spontaneity or freedom. Likewise its use permitted us to make rough statistical comparisons of the experiences in the documents. The writers were not confined in their narration to the items on this guidance form.

Several types of personal interviews were employed in this study. In some instances the personal interview was used as a follow-up and a supplement to the written life history. In a number of cases, as in the instance of ex-

---

[1] See forms in appendix.

convicts, it was through the personal interview that the motion-picture life history was secured—that is, the story was written down by the investigator with the coöperation of the subject. In a number of instances a full stenographic report was made of the interview, the record containing both the questions of the interviewer and the responses of the subject.

Finally, considerable materials were secured through the questionnaire. These schedules were constructed, on the whole, after a study of the recurring items of experience in the autobiographical documents and after consultation and communication with recognized authorities in the field of criminology. The questionnaires were employed largely to ascertain approximately what proportions of given populations were influenced in given ways, and tabulated results were inserted into the report usually only where the life-history materials clearly showed the presence of given types of motion-picture influences in the experiences of individuals.

The materials for the first problem, namely the rôle of the motion pictures in the lives of delinquents and criminals, were secured from the following sources:

(1) About 300 young criminals in a large state reformatory, most of them from 16 to 24 years of age. One hundred ten questionnaires, 258 brief essay documents, and 40 motion-picture life histories were secured.

(2) 55 ex-convicts, many of them on parole. They ranged from 19 to over 31 years of age, most of them being from 25 to 30 years of age. Motion-picture autobiographies were secured.[2]

[2] These were obtained through the services of a trustworthy and capable ex-convict who through his important position as a trusty at the institution had been able to win the confidence and appreciation of many of the inmates. This confidence is reflected in the coöperation of the ex-convicts in granting interviews and narrating their life histories.

(3) About 300 girls and young women delinquents in a large state training school, ranging from 13 to 28 years of age, most of them being 16 to 18. Two hundred fifty-two schedules were obtained, 118 brief essays on the rôle of motion pictures in their careers, and 50 motion-picture life histories.[3]

(4) 20 girls in a truant and behavior-problem school, ranging from 10 to 15 years of age. Motion-picture life histories were secured.

(5) 42 delinquent boys 13 to 15 years of age and 18 delinquent girls 14 to 17 years old awaiting trial. Stenographic interviews were secured.[4]

Supplementary material was secured from the following sources:

(6) 184 grade-school boys and 146 grade-school girls, most of them 12 to 15 years of age, in high-rate delinquency areas [5]; 181 boys and 208 girls mainly 11 to 14 years of age, in medium-rate delinquency areas; and 75 boys and 81 girls mainly 11 to 13 years of age, in low-rate delinquency areas, all in the city of Chicago. The sample was drawn entirely from the sixth and seventh grades. Questionnaire and essay material were secured.

(7) 139 boys in a truant and behavior-problem school, most of them 13, 14, or 15 years of age. Questionnaire and essay materials were obtained.

(8) 90 boys, including both delinquents and non-delinquents, resident in an area in Chicago with the second highest rate of delinquency in the city. The boys ranged

---

[3] These were secured by a woman, trained and experienced in investigation.

[4] Difficulties, for a variety of reasons, of getting opportunity to interview inmates of the penal institutions have interfered with the collection of more autobiographical material. It is felt that more documents than those secured would reveal more distinctly the rôle of motion pictures in the case of certain phases of delinquency and crime.

[5] The schools were selected on the basis of the delinquency rates of the areas in which they were located as compiled by Shaw et al., *Delinquency Areas.*

from 10 to 21 years of age and were mainly second-generation immigrants of Italian parentage. Motion-picture life histories in the form of interviews were secured.

The materials on the effects on inmates of motion pictures shown at correctional schools, reformatories, and penitentiaries were obtained from:

(1) 122 heads of penal and correctional institutions.[6] Questionnaire materials were obtained from the wardens and superintendents.

(2) The autobiographical data of inmates mentioned above.

(3) Samples of 207 and 40 different questionnaires respectively on institutional motion-picture experiences from male convicts in a state reformatory, and 246 questionnaires from female inmates of a state training school.

Finally, for the third problem, some effects of crime pictures on young high-school boys and girls, samples of 203 boys' and 255 girls' motion-picture life histories were secured.[7]

In the collection of materials the utmost care and attention were devoted to building up rapport and gaining full coöperation of the contributors. The contributors were frankly informed of the purpose of the study so as to leave no room for suspicion of our motives. This is a necessary precaution, especially in the penal situation where the investigator is usually regarded with suspicion, at first, because of his possible connection with the parole board or administration of the institution. It was pointed out that we were interested in conducting a scientific study and the persons interviewed were told that they had an opportunity to give valuable assistance. The anonymous character of the in-

[6] Seventy-one of these were secured by direct mail and 51 through the coöperation of the National Society for Penal Information.
[7] These documents are the same ones used in the volume on *Movies and Conduct*.

formation furnished was stressed, it being made perfectly clear that we were not interested in the identification of individual cases. The contributors were asked *not* to sign their names or register numbers. On the basis of the anonymity of the materials an appeal was then made for frank and unbiased information. It is especially important to note that the impartial character of the study was greatly stressed. It was made clear to all contributors that this study had no "axe to grind," that we were not interested in whether the data were of a positive or negative character.

In the cases of the inmates the interviewed persons were then given the life-history guidance sheet and notebooks and pencils which they took to their cells to write their experiences at their leisure and inclination. They were told, of course, not to consider themselves limited by the guidance sheet but merely to regard it as suggesting the field of experience in which we were primarily interested. They were encouraged to write fully on other materials if they felt them to be at all related to our study.

We were especially fortunate in receiving the autobiographical material in the institutional situation. Apart from some difficulty of access to some of the institutions (due to unrest in penal institutions following riots), and the restricted size of the sample of autobiographical materials resulting therefrom, conditions for obtaining life histories were almost ideal. In the institutional situation the inmate, with time on his hands and the monotony of the routine to endure, frequently welcomed the opportunity to fill the schedule forms or write his motion-picture experiences.

The autobiographical materials obtained from the ex-convicts were obtained by interviewing them in the "field" —their homes, offices, poolrooms, speakeasies, on automobile rides, etc. The confidence of the ex-convicts in their interviewer is reflected in the full, spontaneous, and concrete nature of their documents.[8]

Questions invariably arise as to the validity and reliability of personal accounts of experience. In this study we have sought to avoid the pitfalls which usually confront the collection of such accounts, and the errors which bring their use into disrepute.

Contributions to this study were entirely voluntary—no one was under any compulsion to coöperate. Further, painstaking efforts were made to make clear to all informants that our study was strictly impartial, that we were interested neither in affirming nor in denying a relation between motion pictures and their misconduct. All that was requested, it was pointed out, was an honest statement of experiences with motion pictures so far as these experiences could be traced with confidence. The usual frank, friendly, and confidential relations which were established in the interview and life-history situations helped the contributors to catch this impartial and disinterested spirit of the investigation. There was no occasion for and no evidence of willful and conscious fabrication. As one indication of this, attention might be called to the fact that the major portion of our materials is negative in showing any influence of motion pictures on the delinquent or criminal behavior of informants.

As a further means of guarding against unreliable information, we have used as autobiographical data for this study only accounts of experience of a specific and concrete character. The informants were asked to avoid general statements and conjectures. Expressions of judgment or

[8] Through a happy circumstance it was possible to have the ex-convicts interviewed by a reliable and trustworthy ex-convict with whom the writers were intimately acquainted for a period of over two years. In the institutional situation our interviewer had occupied a position in which he had been able to extend favors to the other inmates and gain their confidence and friendship.

opinion were not accepted as valid data to show the influence of motion pictures. They are introduced into the text only when it is of interest to see what are the *opinions* and *judgments* of delinquents and criminals. In tying down our study to detailed and concrete experiences we have narrowed the range of untrustworthy information.

Accounts were carefully checked for internal consistency. Further, in a number of cases the incidents narrated were checked with official records and no important divergencies were discovered. However, the chief means of checking the validity of experience given in a written document was the comparison of document with document. These documents were written independently of one another. The fact that the run of experiences in these documents coming from diverse sources was substantially similar points, in the judgment of the authors, to the validity of the accounts. It is worthy of note that the materials obtained from ex-convicts under circumstances considerably different from those under which the inmate materials were collected were nowise different in content from the latter.

There is considerable truth to the contention that most persons could not tell even if they wished to what an extent and in what manners motion pictures have influenced their conduct. In so far as persons are influenced by factors of which they are not aware, and in so far as dependence is placed on memory, only *part* of the influence of motion pictures on conduct can be obtained through the life-history method employed in this study. Some attention, however, has been given to subtle, unconscious influences which are not readily observable but which are nevertheless an important part of the total effect of motion pictures. This is borne out by the fact, for instance, as will be indicated in our study, that the percentages of delinquents or criminals who acknowledge being influenced to crime by motion pictures is invariably lower than the percentages who admit specific influences of a type ordinarily associated with delinquent or criminal activity.[9] On the whole, however, the materials in accordance with our instructions to contributors represent concrete instances of conduct in which the place of motion pictures could be shown with confidence. This limitation of our data to specific and clearly remembered instances of experience gives essentially a conservative picture of the influence of motion pictures, and conservatism is perhaps most appropriate in what is meant to be essentially an exploratory study.

Space limitation prevents the presentation of documents showing no motion-picture influence. For purposes of maintaining perspective, therefore, as well as for purposes of information, statistical data showing what proportion of the population ackowledge being affected by certain types of motion-picture influences are included wherever possible.

A word of caution should be given about the significance of the statistical data presented in this report. These statistical data are based on questionnaire tabulations and must be interpreted with great care. *They should not be taken as definitely proved measurements of different forms of motion-picture influences but rather as rough approximations suggestive of a likely extent of such influences.* As opposed to the life-history data, the questionnaire responses are in the nature of opinion and judgment and are subject to the uncertainty and instability which attend such kinds of response. We have sought to guard against this uncertainty

[9] Thus, for example, only about 8 per cent of the male criminals in the state reformatory studied acknowledged that motion pictures which they had seen had influenced their criminal behavior, while 49 per cent admitted that the movies had given them on occasion the desire to carry a gun.

by presenting tabulated results usually only where our autobiographical materials show clearly the existence and nature of a given type of motion-picture influence. Even here, however, they may convey a false sense of accuracy, so the reader is again reminded to regard them merely as distributions of replies roughly suggestive of the extent of different kinds of motion-picture influences. Finally, it is perhaps necessary to caution the reader to guard against interpreting these percentages as applicable to the general population and to remind him that they apply only to the population types sampled.

CHAPTER II

DIRECT INFLUENCE ON DELINQUENCY AND CRIME

THE materials secured in this investigation show that motion pictures may contribute either directly or indirectly to delinquency and crime. We shall reserve for the following chapter the treatment of the indirect influence. In this chapter we shall consider the direct relation of motion pictures to delinquent and criminal behavior, as it is indicated by our data.

First let us consider the direct influence of motion pictures on the behavior of delinquent boys. Of a group of 139 truant and behavior cases in a special school in Chicago (most of them from 13 to 15 years of age), 17 per cent indicated in response to a questionnaire that the movies have led them "to do something wrong." Nine per cent of a group of 184 boys (most of them from 12 to 15) in areas where the rate of delinquency is high, nine per cent of a group of 181 boys in medium-rate delinquency areas (age concentration from 11 to 14 years), and 3 per cent of the 75 boys (age concentration from 11 to 13) in low-rate delinquency areas indicated a similar influence.

These groups seem representative of the respective classes of which they are samples. These figures give us some information on the number of boys, from different backgrounds, who feel that motion pictures have influenced them "to do something wrong." Of course, many of them may have had in mind forms of questionable conduct sug-

11

gested by motion pictures, which still were not serious enough to be classed as "delinquent." The figures should be regarded, then, merely as suggestive. They will serve, however, to introduce us to the problem of the influence of motion pictures on delinquency.

A. MINOR DELINQUENCY

Let us begin with a few autobiographical accounts[1] of some minor forms of delinquency, attributed by their writers to suggestions from motion pictures. These represent some of the kinds of experiences referred to as "doing something wrong." The first account comes from a high-school student, the other two from two young criminals serving prison sentences.

Male, white, Jewish, 17, high school senior.—I remember I saw a picture that gave me a yearning to steal. Once I wanted to go to a show and I didn't have any money. I went to our register and took out a quarter and went to a show. I did this taking in a sly manner just as in the show.

Male, white, Polish, sentenced for burglary, inmate of reformatory.—I don't remember the name of the picture but one time I saw a picture where a bunch of boys turned over an apple cart and ran away with a bunch of apples. A few days later our gang tried the same thing. We succeeded in turning over the cart and grabbing a bunch of apples. Everybody got away except me. The "wop" who owned the cart caught me and kicked me.

The writer of the account given continues with a statement of further experiences which, while of minor significance, show the direct influence of motion pictures.

After seeing a gangster picture all of our gang would get together and plan what we would do when we got older. How

[1] The language in the cases presented throughout this volume has been modified in many instances for publication purposes.

In many instances the titles of motion pictures and the names of motion-picture actors, although in our original materials, have purposely been omitted in the published accounts.

tough we would be, and always carry a couple of guns. And if anybody got hard with us how we would pull out one of our guns and boom! shoot 'em dead. Then after talking all about what we were going to do, we'd go around different neighborhoods and act tough. We'd break windows and put horse manure in bags and throw it at people. If any boy said anything to us, we would all jump on him and give him a good beating, but if some man would come after us, boy! how we'd run. After we did this for awhile it got tiresome and then we would waylay some boy from a different neighborhood. We would stop and if he would show any signs of reluctance we would give him a severe pummelling. Then we would proceed to give him a "general shakedown" and if he had any money on him we would take it away from him, and split it amongst our bunch. If he was unfortunate enough not to have any cash in his pockets we would proceed to strip him until he stood in his birthday suit and then we would tie all kinds of knots in his clothes, give him a couple of swift kicks, and call it a day.

Male, white, Italian, 17, delinquent in high-rate delinquency area.—I began to run wild. I ditched school, got caught. Father licked me, but it didn't do any good and then finally the movies finished me. The gang pictures came out and soon had our bunch standing on their heads. They took on nicknames of the characters in the pictures and it wasn't before long when we went out on raiding parties of chicken coops and small stores and getting away with ease. This encouraged us and we continued and we had pulled off some 35 jobs before we were caught. By this time I had quit school and was just bumming around.

There seem to be many minor acts of delinquency similar in nature to the turning over of the apple cart, the pilfering of a small sum from the cash register, and the raiding of chicken coops, which may be directly linked with motion-picture experiences. Ordinarily, they are regarded as of minor significance by those who commit them and by others; so that, in turn, the rôle of the motion pictures seen is not likely to be thought of as very important. Yet, it is proper to make mention of the trivial manner in which the usual delinquent or criminal career begins—a pattern of development very familiar to criminologists. Success in early and relatively minor forms of delinquency may lead to more serious acts, as in the last account which we have given. Viewed from this angle, the influence of motion pictures, in so far as they do suggest minor delinquency, assumes a different proportion. Because of the difficulty in isolating and revealing this early stage in delinquency, usually overshadowed in the minds of delinquents and of others by his later acts of more serious character, we shall not pay much attention to it.

Let us concern ourselves with more serious forms of delinquency, and begin by giving some brief autobiographical statements from prisoners in a penal institution, which show in a general way how some criminals feel about the influence of motion pictures on their own criminal careers.

Male, colored, 23, sentenced for robbery, inmate of reformatory.— In my opinion it is a bad thing for young boys to go to the movies and see pictures showing men stealing. I saw a picture and thought that I could do the same thing.

Male, white, 20, sentenced for robbery, inmate of reformatory.— Pictures of gangsters enabled me to become one of them. I wanted to show my friends what I could do, but it was no use for I was soon caught and sent down here. I robbed, but in a short time I was caught and that ended my career.

Male, white, 20, sentenced for theft of automobile, inmate of reformatory.—Crime pictures led me to go crooked. Gambling and crook pictures led me to try to be a big shot. Movies have shown me the way of stealing automobiles and the charge for which I am now serving sentence.

Male, white, 20, sentenced for burglary, inmate of reformatory.— I have seen movies since I was eleven years old. When I went to the show I saw the men who needed money. So they got together and they stole a car. When I saw how easy it was done

I thought I would try it. I have gone to the movies and seen lots of men playing the bad part and get away with most of it. I seen the bad guy come through. I said to myself that I would try to do it like he did. I thought if he got by with it, I could. ————— played in the picture. When it was over I went home to plan how I would do it.

Male, white, 22, sentenced for burglary, inmate of reformatory.— The movies in my childhood were the principal cause of my downfall. Not all the pictures I have seen had this effect, as some of the pictures I saw were good. I saw how the bad guy in the movies got money and cops could not catch him. Sometimes I wanted to help the bad guy get away. I had nothing against the good guy. As a young fellow I wanted to play the part of the bad guy in our games. When I saw the movies, I sometimes did just as the bad guy did. Yes, it tempted me to crime and I wanted to be a bold guy and take the part of the bad guy in our games.

Of a sample of 258 inmates of this penal institution 11 per cent felt that the movies had some definite influence on their criminal careers, 75 per cent believed that they were not influenced in this manner, and 14 per cent did not write on this question. Of another sample of 110 inmates in the same institution, 8 per cent indicated that they had seen motion pictures which helped to lead them to commit a crime, 78 per cent indicated that motion pictures did not have such an influence, while 14 per cent did not respond to the question.

To appreciate more clearly how the witnessing of certain motion pictures may conduce to criminal behavior in the case of certain individuals, we should get beyond these general opinions and mere statistical statements. Accordingly we shall give a few autobiographical accounts in some detail to indicate how motion-picture experience may be woven in with other experiences to incite to criminal behavior, and to fortify it.

The following case indicates one manner in which motion pictures influenced criminal behavior. It is significant to note that this young man prior to the incident which he discusses had not participated in crime.

Male, white, 19, safecracking, inmate of reformatory.—In every boy's life there are instances when he wishes he were a "big shot" such as the movies produce. In my uneventful life there is only one instance where the imaginative power won control and impressed me with the thrilling (if you might call it that) side of burglary. The picture I am referring to is ————————, played by —————————. It was a drama of racketeering, with safecracking dominating. It was about a young man who turned on society to avenge the wrong that he thought was given him when younger. He studied patiently how to open safes by an easy, quick, and undetectable manner. He would file the tips of his fingers and turn the combination around slowly, until he heard the tumbler on the inside fall, and until another tumbler fell, until the last one would give and then he would pull the door open, and extract the money, always leaving valuable papers, securities, deeds, and other articles of importance intact. But always he would only prey upon merchants on the larger scale. Once, while in an office (I have almost forgotten the exact ending of the picture) a child of a friend of his was locked in the large vault by accident. Everyone thought the child would suffocate because no one present knew the combination of the vault. Then he took some sand paper and filed his finger to a sensitive point and started opening the vault. It was done in record time, which only saved the child by a few minutes. So that was the reason he was found out, or rather it was found out who ———————— was.

That was the picture that I tried to duplicate. It looked so easy and simple that I really believed myself capable of opening a safe by the methods used in the pictures. So with two acquaintances who had been in trouble before and who suggested we get some money to go to Detroit, Mich., on, we set out with tools to open some safe. (By the way, the other boy thought I couldn't do it without tools, which was right.) We picked a consolidated school, which was not near town and in which I thought no one was likely to come around. But much to my embarrassment, I found what an utter fool I must have been in the others' eyes when I tried to open the safe. But we tried it with tools and if I may say so were darn near successful. But it happened that the janitor came to clean up, which was on Saturday morning after a school play the night before, and heard us up in the superintendent's office. He at once went in search of some policemen and returned with four officers, and came in on us. We gave in readily enough and were marched down to the city jail and that morning bound over until the grand jury met. So thus ends what I thought to be a perfect crime.

It is evident that motion pictures were not the only influence leading to the committing of this crime. The writer himself is aware of this when he states:

I cannot wholly blame the movies for that, as the two boys I was with enticed me as much as the movies.

And he indicates still another factor when in another portion of the document he says:

I think that my desire to have a good time and good clothes were the chief factors in my getting in trouble. I always wanted to look just a little better groomed than the next fellow; and so in doing it I had to have money.

The influence of his companions who had previously committed crimes, his desire "to have a good time and good clothes," and his impulses aroused in witnessing this picture seem to be the major reasons for his participating in this particular crime. It is significant to record, incidentally, that his desire for a good time and good clothes was traced by him in a large measure to motion pictures.

Naturally movies were the cause of my failure because I would see clothes and luxury in pictures and would try to have the same or as near the same as those on the screen. . . . So in order to have all those I had to have money, and that is why I tried to break open the safe.

Furthermore, the importance of the movies as a factor in his criminal behavior is evident in his statement:

> It looked so easy and simple that I really believed myself able of opening a safe by the method used in the picture. . . . I believe it was the way he got the money so easily that made me try.

The experience of this individual in showing the influence of a specific motion picture suggests how motion pictures may contribute to criminal activity.

B. Account of One Criminal

The following document written by a Negro inmate of a penal institution shows somewhat more decisively the rôle of motion pictures in feeding a desire to participate in crime and in providing a series of crime techniques. We are quoting his account at some length. First he tells us of his entrance into a gang:

Male, colored, 22, burglary, inmate of reformatory.—I started my criminal career in 1924 when I moved from F—— Street and E—— Avenue. I moved to T—— and C——. I was going to school at F—— Street and C——. There used to be a bunch of boys that came around the school every day about noon time and when school let out, they used to take the boys' school money. If the boys would not give up their money, they would all jump on the poor boys and beat them awful. One day when I was coming out of the school entrance to go and get my lunch across the street in the basement, a gang of boys stopped me and asked me for a dime. I told them that I only had twenty-five cents and had to get my lunch and a school book. The leader of the boys said to me, "let me see the quarter." I took the quarter out of my pocket and showed it to him. He grabbed it out of my hand and started to run. I started to run after him, but his gang grabbed me and beat me up. I went home and told three of my brothers what had happened. They said they would be around the school the next day. The next day around school before my brothers came, I met the same boys. The leader walked up to me and said, "here is your quarter, kid, I was just playing a joke on you." But I found out later that one of the boys in his gang told him that I had a bunch of brothers. He made friends with me and asked me to come around with him some time. I said I would. My brothers told me not to run around with the bunch. If I had taken that little warning I wouldn't be writing this outline now. I started to running around with them after school. Finally I started to bumming school to run around with them.

Next we see the gang attending the movies and receiving from ———————— techniques of criminal behavior which they imitated.

I had never pulled a job until I saw ——————— in ——— ————————. I saw how he broke into a store and robbed a safe and how he picked people's pockets. When we came out of the show a couple of the boys suggested that we try to rob a store, the way we had seen in the picture. We all agreed to the suggestion. We went to a five-and-ten-cent store and bought a crowbar and a screw driver, the tools Mr. ——————— used. Then we went to a store; I will not give the address of the store, but it was a clothing store on F—— Street near C————— Avenue. I put the crowbar a little beneath the lock and bent it back. The other boy put the screw driver on the lock and sprung the lock. We went in and took as many clothes as we could carry.

Having succeeded in their first burglary imitated from the picture, they decide to continue such behavior.

After we had sold what clothes we could not wear, we all decided that would be our racket. There were five of us. I was the oldest and did most of the commanding. After I saw how easy it was to get into stores with double locks or a Segal lock, I started to go by myself. I made more money than the rest of the boys. They all wanted to run with me. When they went with me I gave orders; if they did not like my orders I would tell them to go on home. But they always stayed because they knew whenever I went out to get some money I always came back with some. We robbed a number of stores on F—— Street using the way we had learned.

The motion pictures continued to be a source of instruction in crime and we find the group purposely attending pictures "to find out some other way of robbing places."

> Whenever we saw that a gangster picture was playing at a theater we would all go to find out some other way of robbing places. One day while we were coming back from the Field Museum we saw that ——————— was playing in ——————— at a show at H——— and S—— Street. We saw how he went into a store and cut the burglar alarm wire. Then he came back that night and broke into the store and got away with a bunch of fur coats. We thought we would try that trick. So that afternoon we went out to F—— Street and the elevated to a haberdasher's store. We went in the store and pretended that we wanted to buy something. While two of the boys were looking at some articles, I cut the wire that ran down the side of the door. Then after I had completed my job, the boys told the salesman that they would be back. That night when we went back to the store to rob it, we waited until everybody was out of sight on the street. We went to the back of the store and took the crowbar and started to open the door. When we got the door halfway open, the alarm started to ring. We ran and left it ringing. I guess the man had discovered that the wire was cut when he went to close up the store.

In the above incident we find a criminal technique imitated but without success.

Other techniques of burglary are acquired from the motion pictures after he continues his criminal career.

> I saw another picture at H——— and S—— Street, in which I got an idea how to rob a store. The title of the picture was ———————. I cannot recollect the name of the leading character. It was a picture about some thugs robbing a bank. They tried to get in the door but it was adequately locked. They tried the back but it was the same as the front door. Then they tried the roof but it was well barred with iron bars and screens. Then one of the thugs suggested that they break the lock on the iron door that runs around the outside, then paste some

fly-paper on the window: about ten pieces was what they put on the window. Then they took a hammer and hit around the edge of the fly-paper until the window was broken. When they took the paper down the pieces of glass came down with the paper and did not make any noise. Then they went in the bank and looted it and got away safely without anyone seeing them or hearing them. About a week after I saw the show, a couple of boys and myself tried the trick and it came out successfully. We went out to F—— Street and P—— Avenue. We went up on the roof of a store and pasted paper all over the skylight. Then we hit around the top of the paper lightly. When we took the paper off some of the glass came off with it. Then we took our hands and took the rest out with care. The owner of the store had burglar alarm wires all across the inside of the skylight. We touched one of them and the alarm started to ring. We ran down the alley and hid. About 2 or 3 minutes later the alarm stopped ringing. We went back and squeezed the smallest boy that was with us between the wires. After he got in he knocked a hole in the side wooden door and we went in. If we had opened the door the burglar alarm would have rung. We looted the store and got away safely. I have tried that trick on quite a few stores and it has come out successfully each time. I have never been caught in the act of robbing a place. I have been locked up a number of times. I was always put in jail when someone would tell on me or the police would pick me up on suspicion. I have gone to the Boy's School for little things such as being bad in school, riding in stolen auto, etc.

Motion pictures were one of the chief sources of information on techniques of crime for this delinquent and his gang. His success in learning usable techniques of crime through motion pictures led him to seek in other sources information on ways of burglary. The following account is of one of these experiences.

I read a gangster book, the name of the book was "The Blue Boy." It was about how a thug and a girl thug robbed a jewelry store window with a window cutter. They started off picking people's pockets until they could not make any money. While they were in their flat on the outskirts of the city, the woman was reading a magazine, when she turned to a page that was advertising jewelery. It had a window cutter at the top of the page. She got an idea from that page; she called her partner and told him of her idea. He thought that the idea was wonderful. The idea was of taking a window cutter and cutting a jewelry store window. They went down to the business section of the city. They stood in front of a jewelry store window and looked at a few rings and watches that they wanted. When nobody was looking the man took the cutter and cut a small hole in the window. Then he took watches and rings and handed them to the lady. She put them in her pocket and went away and left him by himself. He met her later at the little flat on the outskirts of the city.

After I had got a good idea how he robbed the window, I thought it would be a good idea. I went in my closet and put on a pair of overalls and went to the five and ten cent store and bought a window cutter. I went around the pool room and got some boys to go with me. I did not see the boys that I wanted so I decided to go by myself. I went around to the back of the pool room and climbed up on the elevated and caught the train and went out to F—— Street. I walked around for a while to find out which jewelry store I wanted to rob. I finally spotted out the one I wanted to rob. It was about 3 o'clock in the afternoon. I thought that was too early so I waited around until around five o'clock. I went over to the window and took out my cutter. I got a little afraid and I said to myself if they caught me I would only go to the Cook County School for Boys for three months because I was only 16 at the time. I took the cutter and pretended that I was looking in the window. I took my time, which was about ten minutes, to cut a small square about 6 by 6. I had already made up my mind what I was going to grab. After the hole was in the window I stood there a couple of minutes to see if everything was all right, I stuck my hand in the window and grabbed a tray of rings. Then I grabbed some watches. I ran around the back of the elevated and started to climb up. A man came running after me. When I got half way up, he started to climb after me. He said, "I saw you take them watches out of that jewelry store window"; then he said "If

you don't give me some, I am going to put the police on you."
I was glad he said that, so I threw him down a watch and said,
"How is that." He said it was alright and went on his way. I
got the train and got off at F—— Street and went around selling
the loot. I had about five hundred dollars' worth of jewelry. I
sold some of the jewelry for fifty dollars. The rest I carried home
and hid. I gave my mother a ring and told her I had been paying on it for a long time. Then I gave my father a watch and
told him the same lie. I gave my oldest brother a watch
and told him that I found it on the seat of a street car, and I
gave my oldest sister a ring. I had run out of lies; so I told her
not to ask any question or I would take the ring back. I hid
the rest in my room. Later on I had older fellows to pawn them
for me. I told the boys around the pool room what I had done.
They said that was a good way of making money. About a week
after I had pulled that job, three of us met at the pool room
about noon. We went in the back and made our plans how we
were going to rob the jewelry store across the street. About
two o'clock we went over in front of the store and stood in front
of the window. When we thought nobody was looking, I took
the cutter and started to cut the window slowly. When I had
finished I put my hand in and took what I wanted. I told the
other boys to get theirs. They tried to beat each other putting
their hands thru the window. The owner of the store across
the street from the jewelry store saw them scrambling at the
window. He started to run over there. I was standing at the
alley and I told them to come on quick. They started to run
toward me. I ran up the alley. The man started hollering,
"Catch them." Some stranger grabbed one of the boys, the
other one kept running behind me. We ran to F—— Street and
I—— Avenue, and caught the elevated and went down to the
loop and went in a show. When we came out it was around five
o'clock. We went back out south, but we did not go around
F—— Street until after dark. When we went around the pool
room the boys told us that the police had been around there with
our other partner looking for us. I gave the other boy 2 rings and
one watch and kept two rings and two watches for myself and told
him that I would see him later and told him to stay out of the
way of the police. Then I went home and one of my brothers told

me that the police had been there two times looking for me. I quickly changed clothes and got out of the house. I went out to F—— Street and met a boy that is down here now and told him all that had happened. He told me that I could stay at his house as long as I wanted to.   He and I went and sold the 2 rings and one watch. He pawned the other in a pawn shop. I gave him three dollars and told him I would be at his house that night. Then I went home and hid thirty in my room.   I gave my mother five dollars and that left me twenty dollars and some change.   I stayed at the boy's house (who is down here now) until the police stopped looking for me. The boy that they caught was sentenced to the St. Charles School for Boys for a year and a half.

As we follow his story we find that motion pictures continue to play a dominant rôle in his career and furnish patterns for a new type of criminal activity.

I saw another picture a year or two before I came down here. If I am not mistaken the name of the picture was ——————. I cannot remember the name of the star character. The character was a young man about 25 or 24.   His people were in a state of destitution; he was out of work; his father was out of work; and his mother was sick.   He had a small brother and sister.   He had tried hard for a job but to no avail.   One day while he was around a pool room he heard some boys about his own age talking about a job they had pulled off. Each of them had a large roll of money. That inspired him to try the same racket. He went to a friend of his and borrowed a gun. He went out that night and stuck up a rich couple in their car. He went home and gave some of the money to his father and told him that he had a job working nights and had drawn on his salary. He went along for a long time robbing people and taking care of his family. One night he went to stick up a taxi driver; he was caught in the act by a policeman. When he went to jail he told the judge why he had committed the crimes. The judge was going to give him a light sentence in jail when a rich man stepped up and told the judge that he would give the boy a chance if the judge would place the boy in his charge. The judge gave the boy a good talking to and turned him over to the man. A few years later he was successful and married. I did not pay that part any attention. I wanted to get some money at the time I was looking at the picture. So I went home and stole my father's pistol out of his writing desk and went down to F—— Street.[2]

I met a boy who is in the Joliet prison now. His name is K——. I told him that I had a pistol and did he want to go with me to make some money. He said that he would but he had never stuck up anybody before. I told him that I had never stuck up anyone either, but I knew how. So that ended. We caught the elevated and got off at ————————; then we walked a few blocks east until we got to a dark street. We walked down the street until we found a gangway. When we had found one we sat down in a window and waited. A lady was the first person that came by the gangway. K—— said, "Let's get her"; I told him no, because women did not carry anything in their pocket-books but keys and cosmetics. A couple of men came by but we did not bother them because they looked like they did not have anything. Finally a well-dressed man came by. I walked out behind him and put the pistol in his back and told him to put up his hands and not to make any noise. If he did I would blow his brains out. He stood still. I told him to come in the gangway. He obeyed. I held the gun on him while K—— went in his pockets. When K—— took his watch, the man said, "Please do not take my watch. My mother gave it to me before she died. I have had it for eight years." K—— asked me should he give it back. I told him yes. The man thanked us. I told him to walk down the alley for a couple of blocks, then we went over and caught the elevated. We went in the back and counted the money. We had got thirty-three dollars and some change. I told him not to tell anyone how we got the money. When we got to F—— Street I hid the pistol back of the pool room, then we went in and started to show the other boys our money. We told them that we had won it in a crap game. I went to the bank next morning and put some of the money in. I always put money in the bank when I would make enough. When the bank at

[2] It is interesting to note the confidence with which he approaches this new crime—robbery with a gun—although he has had no previous experience of this kind. The motion pictures furnished the pattern of behavior so that he felt he "knew how."

———————— closed, what little money I had in there I lost. So you see can that I did not get much out of my crimes.

The first holdup imitated from the movies having been successful, the pair continued their ways:

K—— and I met the next night. We decided that we would work out north. We got off the elevated at L—— and B——. We walked east about a block, then we went north a couple of blocks until we got to a gangway. We saw a man coming down the street. We got ready for him and pulled down our caps and put up our coat collars. I went out behind him and told him to put up his hands and not to make any noise, the same way I had done the first man we stuck up. He told us to take the money and not to take his watch. When K—— was going through his pockets the man coughed. I thought he was trying to make a break for a gun. I almost shot the man. I told him to walk straight ahead and not look back. K—— and I ran through the gangway then down an alley to the elevated. We caught the elevated and went on the back and counted the money. We had four ten-dollar-bills, a two dollar bill and six one-dollar bills and some change. I got off at T—— Street and I—— and told K—— that I would meet him around the pool room the next day.

After this second robbery we find the writer suddenly becoming aware of the seriousness of his behavior. The fact that he almost shot the man when he coughed "because he feared he was trying to make a break for a gun" makes him aware of the possible consequences of his behavior.

When I got home I went in my room which I share with one of my brothers and thought how I had almost wounded a man or killed him. I said to myself if I had killed the man and got caught I would have to pay the death penalty or life imprisonment. I thought for a long time. Then I said I would not try that racket any more because I would sometime run up on some fellow who would try to resist and there I would have to save myself by wounding or taking his life. When I told K—— that

I wouldn't go with him any more and told him why, he told me that I was yellow. I told him if he had killed a man I would be in it just as much as he would. He went and got another partner and I quit the racket. He and his partner are now in the Joliet prison for robbery and attempt to kill with a pistol. I am glad that I quit in time. I have 1 to 10 years for larceny, and he has 1 to life. I know that I will get out and get a discharge a long time before him.

The writer of the document thus brings to a close his account. It is interesting to note that his partner whom he initiated into robbing with a gun continued that form of crime until apprehended and imprisoned in the state penitentiary. This suggests how an idea of criminal behavior presented in a source such as motion pictures may become the starting point of a more elaborate pattern, which may then be transmitted to others.

The case given is interesting in showing how motion pictures may act on the career of a delinquent or criminal. Obviously, the delinquency which we see, in this case, developing into more serious forms cannot be ascribed solely to motion pictures. Criminal behavior is much too complex to be explained by any single factor. Usually it arises from a combination of circumstances and experiences. Such has been true in the case given. It is easy to detect in this case, however, the strand of motion-picture experience, sometimes of negligible import but sometimes of dominating significance. In providing suggestions to crime, in stimulating a certain amount of boldness and confidence in the execution of new crimes, and in providing detailed techniques of crime, motion pictures operated directly on the criminal behavior of this individual. It is interesting and important to see how this boy sums up his own case:

I think that the movies are mostly responsible for my criminal career. When I would see a crime picture and notice how crime was carried out it would make me feel like going out and looking for something to steal. I have always had a desire for luxury and good clothes. When I worked the salary was so small that I could not buy what I wanted and pay the price for good clothes. When I would see crime pictures I would stay out all night, stealing. I have quit six or seven jobs just to steal.

C. FURTHER INSTANCES OF MOTION-PICTURE INFLUENCE ON CRIME

Other cases where the informants declare that motion pictures have helped to stimulate them to criminal activity are given. The two following accounts refer to the imitation of crime techniques by two high-school boys, neither of whom was apprehended and who apparently have not continued in their criminal careers.

Male, white, 17, high-school junior.—I absolutely was influenced by a robbery picture once. My friend Jack and I had seen it. The bandit hero drilled the door of a house and stole many of the valuables. We talked it over; and then armed with a brace and bit went over to a fruit store combined with a meat market and drilled out the lock. It worked fine. We got no money but just sausage and fruit. I naturally don't consider it proper to rob a fruit store now. At the time I was very emotional and would do almost anything for a thrill.

Male, white, 16, high-school sophomore.—In the criminal pictures it shows how easy the crooks get away with their criminal ways and at the end it always shows how the crook gets caught. . . . From these criminal pictures I got the idea that I wanted to participate in crime, robbing stores preferably. I have robbed money plenty of times but not large amounts, giving some to beggars, to little children, and keeping a large amount for myself.

The following excerpt from an interview with a 15-year-old boy awaiting trial for a series of burglaries shows the imitation of burglary technique from the movies:

Male, white, 15, charged with burglary.—

Q. Let me ask this question: Can you think of anything that you have imitated from the movies?

A. Well, nothing but breaking open a window.

Q. Did you see that in a movie?

A. Yea, a couple of times I think I did.

Q. How did they do it in the movies?

A. They just took a bar, some kind of a bar, a piece of iron, kind of flat, and put it under the window and raised it. Or they had a glass cutter and cut around the latch and opened it.

Q. Do you remember what movies you saw that in?

A. No, I don't. I know it was at the Crystal.

Q. What kind of pictures were they?

A. It was at the end of a serial.

The following account written by a prisoner shows the dual influence of motion pictures on criminal behavior which appears in some of the instances already cited: First, instilling the desire for fine clothes, automobiles, luxury, and a gay life; and second, the display of a crime technique serviceable to the satisfaction of these desires:

Male, white, 23, sentenced for burglary, inmate of reformatory.— One of the things that caused my downfall was some of the movies I saw which showed how to jimmy a door or window. The name of one of the pictures I saw which showed how to break into a place was ——————. It was about a gang of crooks and how they would break into a place and take the money or what jewels were there; in other words, make easy money.

After I saw the picture I got a feeling that I would like to try it. The ideas I got about easy money in the movies put it in my head that I would like to try it as I always wanted money to be dressed up in good clothes and to look big. The things they show in the pictures I have seen, show how a fellow would break into a place and get enough money to buy a car and some good clothes and it made me feel that I wanted to be dressed up and have a car too.

I learned only one thing from the movies; that is, how to jimmy a window or door open. I have copied this from the movies.

In the study of *Movies and Conduct* attention is called to the experimentation which may be made of forms of behavior copied from motion pictures. This is also true in the imitation of crime techniques. This experimental character is evident in the following cases. The first is of a 17-year-old boy who was interviewed while awaiting trial:

Male, white, 17, charged with burglary.—

Q. How about the movies? Do you think they had something to do with your difficulty?

A. Well, I think that I learned plenty from them.

Q. What did you learn, would you say?

A. Jimmying a window and things like that. I tried to open a safe once, but I couldn't do that.

Q. Did you see that in the picture?

A. I saw that in a picture, so I tried it.

Q. What picture did you see that in?

A. Some funny kind with —————.

Q. How long ago was that?

A. About three months ago.

Q. Do you remember what picture you saw the jimmying of the window in?

A. I don't know if that was in ————— or not.

Q. What did you see in this picture where the jimmy was used?

A. You know, jimmy a window with a little crowbar.

Q. You saw someone do it?

A. Yes, so we bought ourselves a crowbar and used it for a jimmy.

Q. Do you remember in what theater you saw the picture?

A. That was in the Crystal.

Q. What was the nature of the picture in which they tried to open the safe?

A. It was about —————.

Q. Was this girl trying to open the safe?

A. Yes. It was a wall safe, and she listened to hear the ticks.

Q. Where did you see that picture?

A. That was quite a long while ago. That was in the Queen. She always plays in the little shows.

Q. What did you do after you saw the picture?

A. I kept on thinking about what I had seen and in four places I got into I thought I would try and open the safe.

Q. Were they wall safes?

A. No, it was a great big one. I suppose there was nothing but papers in it, but I wanted to see inside it.

The next excerpt is from autobiographical material written by an ex-convict on parole.

Male, white, 25, sentenced for burglary.—One night after coming from the doctor's office we went to a show and I don't remember the name of the picture; maybe it was one of those "Jimmy Valentine" pictures. Anyway, it showed where a man was searching for "secret panels" in the wall. He'd touch posts and look behind pictures. He touched a molding and a section of the wall opened up. I did get an idea there. I thought maybe one of these big houses would have one and I'd investigate in the next houses I got into.

I walked up M—— to T—— Street, and as Fate does, it gave me the idea to go back and look over the house on the corner. I went home and I went to bed, but not to sleep. I thought of the house, and I had a mental picture of it and all I had to do was go there and find it.

The next morning I left home after breakfast and went over and got into the house. I worked all day. Tapping walls and trying posts, mouldings, shelves, etc., without success. About 4 o'clock I gave it up.

I was dirty from head to foot and went into one of the bathrooms to wash my face and hands. As I was washing myself I looked around for something to dry myself with and went to a place that looked like a linen closet. I opened the door and what should stare me in the face but a big black strong safe. Now that I found the secret hiding place, what could I do about it? I left the place, satisfied; at least I had found what I went after.

Finally, the case of an inmate of a school for delinquent boys:

Male, white, 15, sentenced for burglary.—In the movie some-times I would learn some hints that would help me in crime. In —————— I saw how the robber locked the door from the inside with a pair of tweezers. Then I went home and tried the same thing to see if I could do it later in case I needed to. Then there was another picture, I forget the name, how a fellow opened a locked car with a pipe. He stuck the hollow end and gave a pull and opened the door. It helped me do that plenty of times. I used to think a guy could not get in a locked car unless he had the key or broke the window. But later when I hung around some gang I saw how they broke the lock with a house rock. Then I tried it with the pipe.

Then I saw how a burglar broke in a house with a jimmy. The way he jimmied the window and how he got in and how he jimmied the door to the dining room and robbed all the silver in there, and just as he was going out of the window again a cop saw him and he arrested him and right then and there he con-fessed almost 30 robberies. I don't see how or why a guy should confess all his robberies when maybe he can get off with this one.

Sometimes I would see a show like ——————. It showed how the fellow got away in a fast car. So when I got out I was bold and wanted to do something big. I wanted to steal a car—a fast car—and pull some job with it, but I didn't do it.

We see in these last three cases that crime techniques were observed and efforts made to imitate them with vary-ing success. In one case the techniques were practiced for future use.

D. FURTHER INSTANCES OF IDEAS OF CRIME

Other instances of the copying of forms of delinquency or crime are contained in the autobiographical material secured from delinquents, prisoners, and ex-convicts. We are giving a few of these additional accounts to illustrate how motion pictures may furnish ideas of crime.

Male, white, 15, inmate of state training school.—Not long ago I left home and rented a two-room apartment; two rooms and a kitchen. The apartment was already furnished. I got that idea from the movies. While I was there I got hold of a gun and I wanted to go out and hold up people. Then I thought about that being too risky so I decided I would get a gang together and let them do the holding up and use my apartment for a hangout. I had seen pictures to that effect.

Male, white, Jewish, 18, robbery and rape, inmate of reformatory.—There was a great deal in pictures which showed me about pulling jobs. One picture I saw was —————— with ——————. This picture was of a gentleman crook and how he beat the law. When I see a picture of a big shot—that is if he is the hero—I wish I was in his place. I've seen lots of pictures of fooling the police, pulling safe jobs, and got a bunch of ideas from them. I have copied some of their ways. I found out how to jimmy a window and open a safe.

Male, white, 23, sentenced for burglary, inmate of reformatory.— I learned from the movies the scientific way of pulling jobs. Leave no finger prints or tell-tale marks.

Male, white, Polish, 20, sentenced for robbery, inmate of reformatory.—Of all the crook pictures I have seen throughout my life, there is one thing that I have learned from them and that is, the gun toter with the gun in hand is the smart guy or tough yegg. When he has a gun or several in his hands, he has society at his command. If such a yegg is in need of cash, a gun in hand and a threat with "hands up" is all that is needed to bring him his blood money.

Male, white, 21, sentenced for robbery, inmate of reformatory.— I've learned quite a few ideas of making easy money from moving pictures, such as how a crook acts and what he does after he holds up a person and takes his money away from him. About everything I know was partly through seeing picture shows because pictures give a kid plenty of education in life experience. It shows how people act and how society and other classes of people spend their time. The first stick-up I ever saw was in a movie show and I've seen how it's done and what the crook usually does after the stick-up.

Male, white, 16, sentenced for burglary, inmate of state training school.—In breaking in a store we learned from the movies to use a glass cutter and master key and one boy had a jimmy. If the key didn't work we would use the glass cutter and if that didn't work we would use the jimmy. We would put the jimmy by the lock and force it open.

Male, white, 24, sentenced for robbery, inmate of reformatory.— In some ways we learn a few things about crime from the movies and we get pretty good ideas of how we should act and the things we should and could do in an emergency. They use their guns a lot—mostly machine guns now (anyone that craves excitement in crime likes to have automatic and shot guns and if they are big enough or up in the bucks he will want a machine gun). We get an idea of how to use these weapons and blackjacks, brass knuckles, and bombs too.

Ideas for eluding the police as depicted in the movies are also imitated. Following is an account written by an inmate of a school for delinquent boys:

Male, white, 19, sentenced for robbery, inmate of state training school.—We were in a robbed car while being chased by the police. We pulled into an alley as shown in the movies and waited until they passed us; then backed out, turned around, and went in the opposite direction.

These accounts should convey some understanding of how gangster and crime pictures may suggest "techniques" or ways of committing crimes. More detailed attention is paid to this point in the following chapter. The accounts are used here to illustrate some of the ways in which motion-picture experience may work directly into criminal behavior. In the use of these autobiographical accounts no attempt is being made to convey the impression that the mere witnessing of crime techniques, as they are portrayed in the movies, leads to their imitation. The explanation of imitation is not so simple. Many of the writers of the accounts which we have given were already disposed towards crime; but the techniques which were observed offered some promise of successful use. A reasonable interpretation is that they furthered and fortified the development of criminal conduct. It is of interest to note that such an interpretation is suggested by several of the criminals themselves.

E. SIGNIFICANCE OF THE ACCOUNTS

Let us explain briefly the general significance of the material presented in this chapter. It has been given to show how the witnessing of certain kinds of motion pictures has contributed directly to criminal or delinquent behavior in the case of certain individuals. The skill and cleverness with which a form of crime may be carried out in a picture; the adventure and the thrill surrounding the act; the power and importance of the criminal or gang leader; the enjoyment of money and of high and fast life, frequently shown as an integral part of criminal life—these, separately or in combination, it seems from the accounts, may incite certain individuals to criminal or delinquent behavior. Such motion-picture experiences are, of course, not the sole factors. (It is scarcely conceivable that any instance of criminal behavior could be traced to a single factor.) Yet they take their place alongside of other influences, being sometimes of minor importance, and occasionally of major importance. Frequently they have a different importance in different periods of the same criminal career.

In the light of remarks we may mention again the numerical information given earlier in the chapter, to wit, that, approximately, 10 per cent of the 368 male criminals giving their motion-picture experiences believed motion pictures to have had some direct effect on their criminal careers. While other forces also played on their lives, motion pictures were regarded by them as of noteworthy contributory influence.

While the rôle of motion pictures in leading directly to criminal behavior is not small, it seems to be overshadowed in importance by the indirect ways in which it may dispose boys and young men to delinquency and crime. Some idea of this more extensive scope of the influence of motion pictures should be yielded by the following statistical information.

In response to questioning, 49 per cent of the sample of 110 inmates of a penal institution indicated that movies give one the desire to carry a gun; forty-three per cent think that the movies do not exert such an influence; while 8 per cent did not express an opinion. Twenty-eight per cent of the sample indicate that the movies give one the desire to practice stick-ups; 42 per cent think that they do not exert such an influence; while 30 per cent did not express an opinion on this point. Twenty per cent indicated that the movies have taught them ways of stealing; 34 per cent declared that the movies did not have such an influence; while 46 per cent did not respond to the question. Twenty-one per cent stated that the movies have taught them how to fool the police; 32 per cent indicated no such influence; while 47 per cent did not respond to the question. Twelve per cent of the group stated that they planned to hold up someone or to pull a job when they saw an adventuresome, bandit, burglar, or gangster picture.

These statistical data give an interesting picture of the judgments of a set of representative young criminals. One should note the high proportion who declare that motion pictures stir up desires to carry a gun and to practice "stick-up," that they teach ways of stealing and eluding the police, and lead to the planning of holdups and the "pulling of a job" by reason of their thrilling, adventuresome, and suggestive character. This proportion far exceeds the number of those who acknowledge doing specific acts of crime as the result of motion pictures. The difference indicates that many impulses and ideas of crime are aroused in the mind of the individual by motion pictures, without coming to immediate expression in criminal behavior. Ideas and impulses are checked, they are held within the mind for the given time, being confined, so to speak, to mere incipient activity. In the course of time they may pass away, without leaving any trace; but they may also work in subtle ways into a pattern of life. This sets the problem of the indirect ways in which motion pictures may lead to criminal behavior—the problem to which is devoted the following chapter.

CHAPTER III

INDIRECT INFLUENCE ON DELINQUENCY AND CRIME

A. "Easy Money" and Luxury

To many, the forms of life shown in motion pictures are romantic and alluring. Some people may merely entertain the pious hope or wish to share the life shown; others may be envious of it; but others may be impelled positively to seek and enjoy such life. In the experiences of criminals, delinquents, and marginal delinquents the appeal of a life of wealth and ease is particularly well marked; and the rôle of motion pictures in making this life alluring seems to be quite significant. No point need be made of the ways in which motion pictures may play up a life of wealth and ease, of freedom and adventure, and of power and popularity. Ideas and images of such experiences, as they have been formed through the witnessing of motion pictures, seem to play a conspicuous rôle in the lives of a significant number of criminals and delinquents. It is to this matter that we wish to devote ourselves.

The rôle of motion pictures in stimulating desires for easy money and luxury is evident in the following autobiographical accounts. The accounts are from criminals serving sentence, from ex-convicts, and from a few boys coming from delinquent surroundings.

Male, white, Polish, 23, sentenced for burglary, inmate of reformatory.—The ideas that I got from the movies about easy money were from watching pictures where the hero never worked but seemed always to have lots of money to spend. All the women would be after him and usually there would be two or three women who have a fight over him. They'd pull each other's hair and all that sort of thing. I thought it would be great to lead that kind of life. To always have plenty of money and ride around in swell machines, wear good clothes, and grab off a girl whenever you wanted to. I still think it would be a great life. After seeing these pictures I would think how great it would be if I could get hold of a few hundred thousand dollars and travel all over the world and see everything and have a girl in every city in the world so that no matter where I was I could get lots of loving.

Male, white, 27, sentence for larceny, ex-convict.—Of course, when you'd see cars, many nice clothes, they would make you envious. Why wouldn't they? One would feel the rough goods against his body and think of the grandness of all things that are nice. I guess that is only natural, isn't it?

Male, white, 24, sentenced for robbery, inmate of reformatory.— As I became older the luxuries of life shown in the movies, partly, made me want to possess them. I could not on the salary I was earning.

Male, white, 21, sentenced for larceny, inmate of reformatory.— I don't think gang pictures caused me to be crooked, but I did love to imitate the easy-going young men that starred in them. They had money and fine things and that is what I wanted more than anything else. In society pictures, too, these fine things made me want them more than anything else could. The pretty young girls that played in them caused me to get excited and want to hold them in my arms, but I guess you've got to have money and new cars to get them for awhile.

Male, white, Italian, 16, high-rate delinquency area.—Seeing gangsters having lots of money and big cars and being big shots makes a fellow want them too. When I see pictures of rich people and fine homes, and all that, I just feel that they have it easy.

Male, white, Italian, 14, high-rate delinquency area.—I used to see cowboy and gangster pictures at this time. I didn't like gangster pictures so much but they gave me a big thrill. To see a big gangster, it'd make me feel tough.   Seeing these pictures it would make me feel like having a big car and money and having hideouts like they had.

There would be no point to adding further accounts to show that for many possession of wealth as shown in the movies seems to mean a life of ease, seems to enable one to have plenty of "classy clothes" and automobiles, seems to permit one to entertain girls lavishly, and seems to bring to one power and popularity.   The gayety, the freedom, the luxury, and the "fun" shown as results of wealth, seem to have been a tempting appeal to those whose accounts have been given.   Because of the frequency with which acknowledgments of such experiences are made, it is reasonable to infer that they are true of the populations represented by these individuals.

If individuals come from homes where wealth is limited, where, instead, actual living is closer to a poverty level, the attraction of riches is likely to be all the greater.

Ideas of the Easy Attainment of Money.—If we introduce now the other element in the situation, namely, that motion pictures frequently give the suggestion or impression that wealth may be acquired easily, we can imagine their possibilities in contributing to criminal behavior.   We are not limited, of course, to a mere *a priori* judgment on this point.   Following are a number of autobiographical accounts from criminals and delinquents which show how not only the desire for "easy money" but the idea of its easy attainment may be incited and nurtured by motion pictures.

Male, white, 23, sentenced for burglary, inmate of reformatory.— I got ideas from the movies about easy money.   I felt like I wanted to make easy money as I had seen people in the show make it.

Male, white, 22, sentenced for robbery, inmate of reformatory.—
But it does look easy the way the fellow on the screen does it.
The pictures that they show of this sort show how the man
that is a crook gets his money and how he out-smarts the
law, and it looks very easy. But he cannot always out-smart
the law for too long. It will get him in the time to come no
matter how clever he may be. But at the time I was seeing the
pictures I imagined that I would like to be the guy and get the
easy money.

*Male, white, 19, sentenced for robbery, inmate state training
school for boys.*—Once I saw in a picture two guys in a saloon.
They were betting a lot of money. Then one of the men got
drunk and went away. The man that was sitting in the room said,
"if he stays drunk I will fix it up with that guy so I can win the
bet." The other guy came in a little while and this man that
was sitting in the room began to give him liquor. Pretty soon
they had him drunk and he won the money. I thought that was
a good way to make some money. And in a few years after that
I too did a little of it.

Male, white, Italian, 11, high-rate delinquency area.—Dere was
a man and he used to play dice and he would always win and he
would win lots of money gambling on de horse races. De name
was —————. I felt like I'd like to have dat money myself.

Male, white, Italian, 14, high-rate delinquency area. —————
is a picture about gangsters. They always played dice and
held people up and took the people's money. I felt like I was
one of those and was getting some of the riches they had.
I used to imagine I was a tough gangster and when the coppers
would come I would jump over them and fight them all.

Male, white, 23, sentenced for burglary, inmate of reformatory.—
The ideas I got about easy money in the movies put it in my
head that I would like to try it as I always wanted money to be
dressed up in good clothes and look big. I saw how a fellow would
break into a place and get enough money to buy a car and some
good clothes and it made me feel that I wanted to be dressed up
and have a car.

Questionnaire Responses on Desires and Ideas of Easy Money —Along the line of this discussion, let us introduce the following statistical information.

Forty-five per cent of a sample of 139 truant and behavior-problem boys, 39 per cent of a sample of 184 grade-school boys in a high-rate delinquency area, 29 per cent of a sample of 181 boys in a medium-rate delinquency area, and 19 per cent of a sample of 75 boys in a low-rate delinquency area indicated that motion pictures made them "want to make a lot of money easily."

One should note the increasing percentage of those who speak of this influence, as one compares areas where delinquency is little to areas where it is great. In the areas of high-rate delinquency the absence of wealth is generally greatest, and the opportunities of getting it legitimately are fewest. With such a background the attractive portrayal of wealth, the implication that it may be acquired easily, and the suggestion of ways of securing it quickly are all likely to make a definite impression. This suggests why a given run of pictures may have no noticeable effects on people whose modes of living permit them certain privileges and enjoyments; whereas they may reënforce delinquent inclinations in others who do not have such privileges and opportunities.

Yet it is not true that motion pictures showing lavish wealth and luxury, as in the instance of society dramas, are the kind that arouse desires to make money easily. The pictures that seem to do this are rather those of the "gangster" or "crook" type. The reason for this seems to be due in part to the fact that the themes of such pictures are more familiar to the people concerned, more within their observation of experience. But it seems due, also, to the fact that such pictures suggest definite and feasible possibilities of attaining such wealth. The display of riches in a "society" picture is likely to be remote to the experience of many people; further the picture is scarcely likely to present the impression that such a life may be immediately available. This accounts probably for the significant connection between gangster pictures and desires for easy money. Let us now return to the questionnaire responses.

In response to the inquiry as to what kinds of pictures make them "want to make a lot of money easily," 55 per cent of the truant and behavior-problem boys, 34 per cent of the grade-school boys in the high-rate delinquency areas, 20 per cent of the boys in the medium-rate delinquency areas, and 17 per cent of the boys in the low-rate delinquency areas indicated in free response that pictures of the gangster, fighting, and gun-play types incited such desires. In contrast to this distribution it was found that only 5 per cent of the truant and behavior-problem boys, 9 per cent of the boys in the high-rate delinquency areas, 8 per cent of the boys in the medium-rate delinquency areas, and 12 per cent in the low-rate delinquency areas indicated wealthy or rich type of pictures as provoking them "to want to make lots of money easily." Four per cent of the truant and behavior-problem boys, 2 per cent of the boys in the high-rate delinquency areas, 5 per cent of the boys in the medium-rate delinquency areas, and no boys in the low-rate delinquency areas indicated fast life and sex pictures as arousing such desires. Nine per cent of the truant and behavior-problem boys, 3 per cent of the boys from the high-rate delinquency areas, 9 per cent from the medium-rate delinquency areas, and 7 per cent from the low-rate delinquency areas indicated other types of pictures as creating such desires; while 48 per cent of the truant and behavior-problem boys, 53 per cent of the high-rate area boys, 58 per cent of the medium-rate area boys, and 64 per cent of the low-rate area boys left this question blank, implying apparently that no pictures had such an effect.

Let us now give some data, referring to this discussion, from the responses of a sample of 110 inmates of a penal institution. Forty-five per cent felt that motion pictures developed a desire for easy money; 39 per cent felt that they did not; and 16 per cent did not express themselves on this topic. Forty-five per cent of this same sample feel that the movies suggest ways of getting money easily; 40 per cent feel that they do not; while 15 per cent did not venture an opinion when asked to respond freely. Forty-four of the group, or 40 per cent, indicated specific ways in which the movies suggest making money easily. Of these that indicate specific ways:

```
 1 ( 2%) indicate movies suggest the stock market;
 3 ( 7%)     "      "      "     work;
 3 ( 7%)     "      "      "     "several ways";
 1 ( 2%)     "      "      "     "fast life";
 1 ( 2%)     "      "      "     not working;
11 (25%)     "      "      "     holdups;
 2 ( 4%)     "      "      "     confidence games;
 1 ( 2%)     "      "      "     gambling;
 9 (20%)     "      "      "     crime;
 4 ( 9%)     "      "      "     burglary;
 1 ( 2%)     "      "      "     bribery;
 5 (11%)     "      "      "     stealing;
 2 ( 4%)     "      "      "     bootlegging.
```

It is worthy of note that 35, or 80 per cent, of this sample of 44 indicated that the motion pictures suggested some form of crime as a means of obtaining money easily.

"Easy Money" and Actual Crime.—It is obvious that the creation of the desire for luxury and a life of ease and the suggestion of forms of crime as a means of attaining

wealth and comfort do not necessarily lead to criminal behavior. However, they may do so. We need only to recall one of the cases cited earlier in which motion pictures aroused the desire for a life of wealth and luxury and suggested the opening of a safe as an easy means of satisfying this desire.[1] This delinquent boy makes the following statement:

Male, white, 17, sentenced for safecracking, inmate of reformatory.—I think that owing to my desire to have a good time and good clothes, movies were the chief factors in my getting in trouble. I always wanted to look just a little better, and a little better groomed, than the next fellow, and so in doing it I had to have money. Naturally, movies were the cause of my failure, because I would see clothes and luxury in pictures and would try to have the same or as near the same as those on the screen. I feel sort of odd when with some girls if I am not dressed as good or better than the other fellow and I also want my own car. So in order to have all those I had to have money and that is why I tried to break open the safe.

As further evidence on this point we may present the following accounts:

Male, white, 18, sentenced for robbery, inmate of reformatory.— Knowing that the "bad guy" had plenty of money and an easy way of getting it by robbing or burglarizing, and the good guy was slaving for his money, I thought that the bad guy was the smartest. So I thought I would rather be a bad guy. The play ——————— was a gangland picture and it thrilled me to see gangsters' guns and shooting of enemies, robbing banks, and thinking it was easy I took up robbery as the best means of obtaining money. ——————— played in the picture.

Male, white, 20, robbery, inmate of reformatory.—When I see a movie that shows snappy clothes, big cars, and lots of money, it makes me want to have them too. It makes me ashamed of my own clothes and wish I had clothes like theirs. They also make

[1] See page 16.

me think of how to make a lot of money; for instance by working, but that takes too long. Then it makes me think of sticking up people and robbing them. I tried this but was soon caught and sent down here.

It should be evident from this brief discussion that one manner in which the motion pictures may lead to delinquent and criminal behavior is through inciting desires for luxury, fine clothes, automobiles, and pleasure. Not only may such longings be aroused, but suggestions of achieving them easily may be given, frequently in the form of crime techniques.

Sometimes this combination may lead directly to criminal behavior; more frequently its influence is confined to imagination and yearning. In the end it may work unwittingly to make the individual more susceptible to undertaking crime. Or it may reënforce motives already responsible for the criminal careers of those who are already participating in crime. To recall that of the group of 110 criminals, 45 per cent felt that motion pictures developed a desire for easy money, and that a similar proportion declared also that the movies suggest ways of getting money easily, is to appreciate this indirect influence. While of the 110 only 9 believed that motion pictures contributed directly to their criminal activity, it is reasonable to infer that in many of the others motion pictures were influential, even though the subjects were unaware of such influence.

B. Emotional Possession and Crime

Certain types of motion pictures may indirectly influence delinquent and criminal behavior by inducing emotional possession—a phenomenon which we have considered in another work.[2]

[2] See *Movies and Conduct*.

The chief characteristics of emotional possession may be mentioned here: the inciting of impulses, the arousing of a given emotion, a relaxing of ordinary control, and so an increased readiness to yield to the impulses aroused. These states of mind and feeling come, usually, as a result of the individual "losing himself" in the picture, or becoming deeply preoccupied with its drama or movement. Thus in witnessing a mystery picture, a child may become frightened; in viewing a sad picture, an individual may cry; in seeing a passionate love picture, a young man or young woman may experience a strong impulse to love relations. In the case of delinquents or of criminals, or of those marginal to these types, pictures of excitement, adventure, and daring seem most likely to induce emotional possession, and, in doing so, to give impetus to delinquent tendencies.

A view of the manner in which motion pictures may exercise this influence is given by the autobiographical materials. The first three accounts are presented as illustrations of this form of emotional possession; the others stress more some of the effects on feelings and impulses.

Male, white, 28, sentenced for robbery, ex-convict.—All action pictures excite me—fight pictures especially—sometimes I feel like going up to the pictures and getting into a fight scene where a fellow is getting the worst of it. I go through the motions of hitting and moving my arms and get restless; many times the fellows around me would get a bigger kick in watching me than they would the picture. I wasn't doing it for their amusement; I just couldn't control myself.

Male, white, Jewish, 18, sentenced for robbery, rape, inmate of reformatory.—I would see the "Big Shot" come in a cabaret. Everyone would greet him with a smile. The girls would all crowd around him. He would order wine and food for the girls. Tip the waiter $50.00 or more. After dining and dancing he would give the girls diamond bracelets, rings and fur coats.

Then he would leave and go to meet his gang. They would all bow down to him and give him the dough that was taken from different rackets. When I would see pictures like this I would go wild and say that some day I would be a Big Shot that everyone would be afraid of, and pay big dough, live, like a king, without doing any work.

Male, white, Italian, 14, high-rate delinquency area.—"Gangster pictures show the way dey get bumped off and all dat stuff. You don't tink nottin' about it. You just get a lot of thrill out of it. You wish dat you had his chance to be a big shot and have all his money and power."

Spirit of Bravado.—The following accounts show how feelings of toughness, daring, and adventurousness may be aroused in boys in witnessing stirring gangster, burglary, or bandit pictures:

Male, white, Italian, 16, high-rate delinquency area.—"I never went to shows much. When I went I just went because I didn't have any place to go. I saw de ————————. When I saw dese gangster pictures I kinda felt big and tough like dem."

Male, white, Italian, 10, high-rate delinquency area.—"I never saw a picture dat made me do anything bad. De ———————— made me feel like I was a big tough guy. I felt just like ———————— ————————. I felt just like I was in de pitcher, like I could take a guy and knock him down."

Male, white, Italian, 11, high-rate delinquency area.———————— made me feel like I'd like to be a gangster. I felt like a gangster, bad and big and strong and tough and when we got outside we played ————————.

Male, white, Italian, 10, high-rate delinquency area. ———————— made me feel like a robber. I wanted to be like ————————, big and tough."

Male, white, Italian, 11, high-rate delinquency area.—When I saw ———————— in ———————— I felt like a big gangster. When I got outside I felt strong and tough like the gangsters in the show.

Male, white, Italian, 10, high-rate delinquency area.—When I see an exciting picture I feel like the big shots that know schemes and hiding places and know how to kill and capture cops and get a lot of money. I feel just like one of these guys when I'm outside.

Male, white, Greek, 13, high-rate delinquency area.—I've seen pictures that made me want to be a tough guy. For about a week I'd keep thinking about it and I'd make off I was a big shot. ——————— was the captain of all the gangsters. The cops used to stop them on the highway and he'd tell the gang to give them the works and they'd kill them. A rich guy was going out with his wife and he caught them, but he couldn't do anything, because there were too many coppers around. So he went away and sent the rich guy tickets to a masquerade ball. Then he and a pal came dressed as coppers and took him away, but the rich guy's guards followed them to the hangout. Just as —————— was goin' to kill the rich guy the squad came and shot him. I felt good because —————— had everybody afraid of him. I didn't like the rich guy cause he was yellow, the coppers found him hiding in a barrel when they came to the hangout. I'd like to be like —————— and have lots of money and have people afraid of me.

All of these accounts come from boys living in an area of high delinquency. They seem to be captivated by the daring, adventurousness, and toughness shown in the pictures. Even in narrating their experiences the emotional influence was evident in their increased excitement during the interview, and in their apparent reliving of the scenes.

That such a condition of excitement and aroused feeling is not uncommon, seems to be shown by the following set of questionnaire responses.

Twenty-eight per cent of the truant and behavior-problem boys, 39 per cent of the grade-school boys in the high-rate delinquency area, 32 per cent of the boys in the medium-rate delinquency area, and 31 per cent of the boys in the low-rate delinquency area indicate that exciting movies make them want to do something brave and daring. Thirty-eight per cent of the inmates of a penal institution (sample of 110) found that movies were usually exciting. Twenty-six per cent of this sample indicate that motion pictures taught them to act "tough" or to act like a "big guy," while 32 per cent indicate no such influence and 42 per cent did not respond to the question. If we omit those who did not respond we see that 44 per cent declare that the movies taught them to act "tough" and to act like a "big guy." Of a group of 258 inmates, who have given brief accounts of their experiences, 17 per cent felt that an exciting picture made them feel brave, "tough," and adventuresome; 26 per cent indicated that they were not influenced in this way; 57 per cent did not answer the question. Out of the 113 who responded those who indicated that an exciting picture made them feel brave, "tough," and adventuresome constituted about 40 per cent.

Overt Expression of the Spirit of Bravado.—Emotional possession of the sort of which we have been speaking does not necessarily lead to overt behavior; that is, to the expression of the impulses aroused. But that it may very well do so is indicated by the following instances.

Male, white, 24, sentenced for robbery, inmate of reformatory.—When I see an exciting and adventuresome picture I feel both brave and adventuresome. Usually after such a picture up until about three years ago I felt as though I wouldn't move an inch in order to avoid a fight myself. I would say it brought out the meaner side of me, but it never made me feel as though I wanted to do anything brave or daring outside of a fight.

Male, white, Italian, 11, delinquent boy in high-rate delinquency area.—"I saw a picture of a bad guy shooting a good guy and gettin' a lot of money off him. It made me feel like I'd like to get a lot of money like that. He was husky-like and I felt big and tough like him; and every time I saw a picture of a gangster in front of the show I socked it with my fist."

Male, white, Italian, 10, high-rate delinquency area.—"I feel tough lots of times when I see movies with tough guys in them, and if some guy gets tough with me I sock him."

Male, white, Italian, 16, high-rate delinquency area.————— in ————— made me feel tough like that. He was a tough captain. I tried to imitate him when fellows were around. I'd grab them and wrestle with them just like he did. He'd show his strength to his sailors and I tried to do the same thing.

Male, white, Polish, 15, sentenced for burglary, inmate of state training school.—I saw a play about some gangs having a fight and it showed how they fought. When we got out of the show, we would walk down the streets. When we got down to A—— and R—— we would go in a school yard and start a fight there.

Male, white, Italian, 12, high-rate delinquency area.—I feel brave when I see an exciting picture. Why not? I feel tough and go home and lick my little nephew.

Male, white, Italian, 13, delinquent in high-rate delinquency area.—We went to a show on Madison St. and we saw a crook picture; when we got outside we turned up our coat collars and acted tough like we were stickin' up guys. When I see an exciting picture I get all "nervoused" up. I don't know what to do then. Sometimes I feel big and tough and if a guy comes up to me I bang! punch him in the nose and without even asking what he wants.

Male, white, Jewish, 18, sentenced for robbery, rape, inmate of reformatory.—Whenever I saw a gang-land picture I would come out feeling tough, rough, and hard to beat; and I would beat someone up. One time I saw a picture of this type. I came out of the show and saw the newspaper boy on the corner selling papers who was about the same age as me—twelve. I punched him in the kisser; he fell down and I jumped on him. Some of his money rolled out of his pocket. So I beat him until he went to sleep. Took all his money, $4.99.

Furthermore, the case already cited in Chapter II [3] illustrates very well the action of emotional possession in inciting a gang of boys to act tough, break windows, throw things at people, beat up boys and take their money away from them.

The series of accounts which have been given suggests how easily the emotional condition of excitement and daring may become connected with delinquency and crime. As the cases imply, it is quite common for this form of emotional excitement to express itself in fighting, in acting "tough," or in doing some form of mischief. Some further questionnaire responses may be conveniently given on this point.

Forty-one per cent of the truant and behavior-problem boys, 36 per cent of the grade-school boys in the high-rate delinquency area, and 33 per cent in each of the medium-rate and low-rate delinquency areas indicated that they found fighting as portrayed in the movies attractive and fascinating. Furthermore, 14 per cent of the truant and behavior-problem boys, 14 per cent of the grade-school boys in the high-rate delinquency area, 7 per cent of the boys in the medium-rate delinquency areas, and 4 per cent of the boys in the low-rate delinquency areas indicated that exciting movies made them want to act "tough" and fight someone. Twenty-one per cent of the sample of 110 inmates of a penal institution stated that exciting pictures made them want to do something daring and adventuresome, while 8 per cent indicated that exciting pictures made them want to act "tough" or to fight someone.

Emotional possession not only may lead to mere mischief or mild delinquency, but, it would seem, may dispose individuals to more serious delinquency. Ten per cent of

[3] Pages 12 and 13.

the behavior-problem boys, 4 per cent of the grade-school boys in the high-rate delinquency areas, 3 per cent of the boys in the medium-rate delinquency areas, and 5 per cent of the boys in the low-rate delinquency areas admitted that exciting gangster, burglar, and bandit pictures made them feel that they wanted to be a gangster or burglar. Seven per cent of the truant and behavior-problem boys, 3 per cent of the boys in the high-rate delinquency areas, 2 per cent in the medium-rate delinquency areas, and 1 per cent in the low-rate delinquency areas acknowledged that some exciting pictures made them want to break into a house and take something or to take things from other people.

Some autobiographical accounts will help us to understand these more serious ways in which emotional possession may support crime.

Male, white, Italian, 16, high-rate delinquency area.—After seeing an exciting gangster picture, I feel pretty good and when I get outside I feel like going back in again. Lots of times I feel like going out and holding somebody up.

Male, white, Italian, 11, delinquent in high-rate delinquency area.—When I see a gangster picture I feel much like the big shot himself when I get outside. Sometimes I imagine I'm him. I feel like a big shot then and I'll go out and rob and be a sport.

Male, white, Italian, 11, high-rate delinquency area.—After seeing a movie which showed pictures concerning crime it made me feel like I could steal things without being caught. I think that movies showing pictures of crime make a kid feel bolder. When I see an exciting picture I feel adventuresome.

Male, white, Italian, 21, sentenced for robbery, inmate of reformatory.—Pictures about gangsters enabled me to become one. I wanted to show my pals what I could do but it was of no use. I am down here now and just for trying to be bold. I used to think I was a smart guy, but it never did get me anywhere anyway. Pictures like that used to make me raise my chest out because I thought I was one of them in there. Foolish ideas were put in my head and like a damn fool I followed them out. Whenever I see a tough picture I feel the same way. Yes, I used to go out and stick up people and rob like the fellow in the picture . . . just as long as I had money then I was satisfied.

Male, white, 19, sentenced for robbery, inmate of reformatory.— When I see an exciting and adventuresome picture I usually feel adventurous and feel like doing something daring. A picture that's pretty exciting and adventurous makes me want to do something and when I come out of the show I usually go home and stand around the corner and listen to the other fellows talk till it gets pretty late and when it's between 2 and 3 o'clock in the morning, I would go with another fellow and break into some store that looked like it had a few dollars in it.

Significance of the Spirit of Bravado.—The lesson which seems to be told by this series of cases and those given previously in this section is that a spirit of adventure and bravado may be induced in boys by certain pictures. Wild, daring, and reckless feelings may be aroused; the boys aspire, in their emotional excitement, to be bold, and "tough" and to act like a "big shot." As some of the accounts imply, there is frequently a readiness to act along the line of the feelings and impulses which are aroused. The number of those who acknowledge having experienced such emotional excitement as the result of seeing certain motion pictures exceeds, of course, the number who trace some of their delinquent or criminal tendencies to the movies. Yet one might readily assume that this emotional experience might unwittingly reënforce dispositions to engage in crime, without being particularly noticed by those who have the experience. If it be true that in much delinquency and crime there is a spirit of bravado, boldness, and "toughness," it seems to be not an unreasonable assumption that the inducement of this spirit by motion pictures may help to initiate or reënforce criminal activity. The declaration by some delinquents and criminals that this has been true in their cases suggests that it may be true in others.

Ordinarily the heightened emotion excited by a picture is short-lived. The feelings and impulses which were aroused subside, and there is lost the corresponding readiness to act.[4] Yet in some instances the excitement may become fixed in the form of a persistent tendency to act boldly and with bravado. This tendency may be woven into the dispositions of an individual and may express itself at different points in his career. This represents one of the indirect ways by which motion pictures, in inducing the spirit of bravado, may contribute to criminal behavior.

A Case Showing the Persistence of the Spirit of Bravado.— In the case which follows we see something of this form of influence. The case is an autobiographical account of a notorious criminal and gang leader whose identity must necessarily be kept secret. One can easily detect in the description of his experiences the influence of "Wild West" patterns: the sweep of the gang into the city speakeasy or small-town bank, the shooting of bullets into the air or through the floors and ceilings, and the scattering of silver into the streets. He himself admits the persistence in his feelings of the spirit of bravado originally aroused by "Wild West" pictures. His case with some omissions is now given. Speaking of his childhood play associates he says,

> *Male, white, 38, sentenced for robbery, ex-convict.*—After our gang was reorganized, we went to work for factories and shops in and near the Loop, as messenger boys, machine hands, etc. I was employed in a print shop as a Gordon Feeder and made considerably more money than the rest of the fellows of the

[4] This feature has been more fully described in *Movies and Conduct.*

neighborhood. This afforded us little luxuries, heretofore not indulged in. We were in constant attendance at the neighborhood Nickelodeon. Here I took keen delight in seeing the Indian massacres on the western frontiers, or perhaps a daring holdup of a stagecoach. I sincerely believe that these pictures had a great influence on my life, and on the lives of my companions, which came to the front in later years.

His interest in western themes continues as an inmate of a Federal penitentiary for stealing, forging, and passing Government money orders.

I would obtain most of the "Wild West" stories that were advertised, to the utter disgust of my cell partners. They went in for the "heavier" kind of literature, which I could not even begin to read. They used to lecture me by the hour to get a hold of myself and try to educate myself while I had the chance. We had some of the best pictures, pictures that were playing the big cities at the same time. I would attend, but would be utterly bored by the majority—love scenes or ancient history, pictures which would really make a hit with my cell partners. I would enjoy western pictures or pictures of the sea and storms. They would remark that I had the mind of a kid, and that I never grew up.

After his release from this imprisonment he was determined to make only big hauls or nothing at all. He made connections with a gang through references obtained at the penitentiary and soon became their leader:

I fell in with that "mob" taking orders, and before the year was out I was giving "orders." I declared myself leader one night, when I refused to give the "Heb" a "cut." What right did he have to an "end" when he did not even supply tips, protection, or anything? All he had was a lot of "bluff," and I will admit he had brains and could use them. I told him if he expected anything, that he would have to get out and "hustle" like the rest of us. One word led to another and the fight was on. I guess I done everything but kill him; this increased the respect that the "mob" had for me. I declared myself, by challenging anyone else in the place who resented what I had done, but not a soul took me up. This showed what a bunch of yellow-backed rats I had to deal with.

As a leader "Wild-Western picture ideas came to the front."

I led that "mob" like they had never been led before. We took saloons and poolrooms, places where it required some amount of daring to take the chance of "Heisting" them, because as a rule gunmen and Heist guys hang out in the likes of these places. Now is about the time those wild-west picture ideas came to the front.

We'd drive up to a flying stop in the front of one of these places. I'd alight from the car on the run, gun in hand, and run in and line them up. When the rest of the "mob" would see there was no danger, they would come in, and do the hollering and bluffing, and as a rule they were always willing to do the searching. They were the yellowest rats I ever met up with in my born days.

When we made out-of-the-way saloons, I'd go in, shooting into the floor and up in the air. I got a big kick out of that. One night we met a "hard" customer to deal with. I put my gun in my pocket (giving him a square deal) and was fighting it out with him (I had the best of the argument) when he kicked me in the groin. I was down but not out; I shot the hand right off of that "Dino" Son-of-a ——! My "mob" had disappeared, I was alone, among 25 or 30 bloodthirsty Dinos, gun empty, and hopelessly crippled. I used the butt of that gun, fought, kicked, and bit my way out of that joint; right dead bang into the arms of the "mugs."

I stood "pat," and said that they tried to take my life, disclaimed all knowledge of the gun, said that it belonged to one of the Dinos. They couldn't prove anything on me, and I was found not guilty by a jury in Judge ——'s court.

After being deserted by his gang in the above encounter he left them, made new connections, and organized a new gang. As a leader of this group, patterns of behavior imitated from Wild West pictures are again apparent in his criminal undertakings.

I was mapping out the plan of a new organized gang, and I was their leader. This fitted in nicely with their plans of thinking, and out we went. It was easy and everyone of them done their share. The Irish are a bunch that have a lot of guts and no brains. We "touched" places right and left without a fall, not even a close call, if we had had one I think it would have slowed our pace, but we never did, and on we went. Bolder and bigger hauls each time. The newspapers, police, and everybody was screaming for our arrest. Each day we had a new story of our latest escapade. We were a daring "mob," to say the least.

——— National Bank, we took this in true wild-west fashion. Went into the town shooting, and left every kid in town wishing us luck. We were just getting away—there were fast cars behind us on the chase—and I took a sack of silver and threw it out onto the street. School was just letting out, and you should have seen those kids. You could hear the brakes of those pursuing cars a mile away. If it wasn't for those kids we would have been caught right there and then, and I'll bet killed.

Well, we had a stranger in with us on this, and he talked a little too much to his friends, and now enters the coppers.

They pinched him, and it wasn't an hour before the coppers induced him to lead them to our hangout. There we were, all four of us—caught in a trap, and not an outlet in the world.

We went back to ——— County, and went in front of a farmer jury. The Judge had our sentences written out long before we went to trial. We hadn't a ghost of a chance. Kangarooed right into the "stir," 10 years to life. It was for lots of money, and we got lots of time.

The individual—now an ex-convict—who gives this account adds:

I am sure I never knew fear. I always remembered myself as one of the bold, fearless cowboys. If ever I get a kid, he will never get to see a picture, read a book, or a magazine until the "old wise guy" reads it first. I would much rather see him dead than to see him go through life as I have.

Our materials are not such that we can make an estimate of the number of criminals in whose lives there may persist a spirit of bravado induced originally by motion pictures, as in the case which has just been given. In view of the large number who acknowledge experiencing daringness and boldness in seeing certain motion pictures, it seems likely that the linking up of such feelings with a persistent crime career is not unlikely.

C. Daydreaming and Crime

Another indirect way in which motion pictures seem, from our study, to be connected with crime is in inducing daydreaming or phantasy of criminal behavior. The relation between daydreaming and behavior has never been satisfactorily pointed out, and yet undoubtedly it is important.[5] That motion pictures may incite daydreaming built up around images of crime is clearly evidenced by our study.

Thirty-two per cent of the truant and behavior-problem boys, 32 per cent of the high-rate delinquency area grade-school boys, 24 per cent of the medium-rate delinquency area boys, and 40 per cent of the low-rate delinquency area boys stated that exciting movies made them imagine having a lot of adventure. Of greater import, however, is the content of the imagery. Ten per cent of the truant and behavior-problem boys, 10 per cent of the high-rate delinquency area boys, 6 per cent of the medium-rate delinquency boys, and 5 per cent of the low-rate delinquency area boys indicated that a thrilling burglar or bandit picture made them imagine doing daring things and fooling the police. Twenty per cent of the convicts studied, of a sample of 110, declared that they thought of being gangsters or burglars when they saw an adventuresome gangster, burglar, or bandit picture; and 26 per cent imagined themselves doing big and daring things and fooling the police.

[5] See the discussion on this point in *Movies and Conduct*.

Following are some statements of phantasy in which the individual has imagined himself in the rôle of a gangster or criminal.

Male, white, Bohemian, 15, sentenced for burglary, inmate of state training school.—When I was small I used to be crazy about seeing a copper and robber play. After the play I would go home and act as if I was the robber and sometimes my brother or my chums would be the police. Then later in my years I would break in a store and make off it was a bank or some big place to rob.

In my mind I felt good for the bad guy and always wished he would pull the job and never get caught. I would always take the part of the bad guy and think in my later years I would be some big gangster and be the leader of a big gang. Have a nice home; make off I'm in a business, but have a secret room and tell the gang what to do. To have all the people fear when they hear my nickname and not know my real name. I would also like to baffle the police so that they never would catch me or any member of my gang. And have a gang with all brave guys that would die for me. Do anything I told them to do and no dirty double-crossing in my gang. I would take the double-crosser and take him for a ride and shoot him, with a penny in his hand to show that he was a dirty stool-pigeon.

Male, white, Italian, 16, delinquent, high-rate delinquency area.—When I see a gangster or burglar picture, I figure if they can make money that way so can I. I imagine myself as a gangster and go ahead and try to act the same way they did.

Male, Negro, 14, high-school freshman.—As a result of the movies I would sometimes dream that I was rich or wealthy and would have plenty of money or even a rich mansion and automobile in which wealthy people ride. I would sometimes be tempted to act like some of the movie stars I had seen. Then again I would like to be like some crook who I have seen in some underworld plays. Such as —————— in the ——————. There were, of course, many temptations I have had in seeing a number of these pictures.

Male, Negro, 15, high-school sophomore.—Cowboy pictures, war pictures, fighting pictures and underworld pictures give me new ambitions. I want to be like the star of any of these pictures. Sometimes I would imagine myself being a great gunman. Then whenever a policeman was the star of an underworld picture I would want to become a great detective.

Male, white, 22, sentenced for burglary, inmate of reformatory.— As a child I always wanted to be the bad guy and always wanted to get into the racket and would always lay in bed and think of all the money that the bad guys would make. There were also a few pictures that I saw that caused me to think that I was a bold burglar and I always thought of pulling a job but when I got to the place I always got cold feet. The name of one of the pictures was ——————— starring ———————. Well, after I saw that picture I wanted to make one big haul and then go on easy street for the rest of my life.

Male, white, 20, sentenced for burglary, inmate of reformatory.— When I would see a fellow go in a house and rob, I always thought that it looked easy. So after I grew older I planned to see if I could accomplish some of the crook's jobs. The first picture I saw that led me to think I could accomplish some of the things the crooks did was ——————— starring ——————— and a few other stars. After I saw the picture I went home and studied and planned it out like I would do it if I was going to pull a job. After I had seen a few more crook pictures I had an idea that I would like to be a big guy. I may have got a few ideas from the pictures concerning jobs, but the greatest part of the time I planned my own jobs. I have seen many crooks and many jobs pulled in pictures, but I can't see how they can make a fellow do the same. The picture may give the fellow an idea, but the jobs that are pulled off in the pictures are the biggest part of the time impossible to do. Whenever I saw a crook caught after pulling a job in the movies and how he was tripped up and got nabbed by the police, I always did it the opposite way.[6]

Male, white, 19, sentenced for forgery, inmate of reformatory.— I have seen pictures and imagined how easy it was to steal and cash bum checks and I have done that very thing.

[6] In addition to illustrating how motion pictures may induce criminal imagery, this case suggests how the ways by which the criminal is shown as being caught may be studied so as to avoid pitfalls.

Male, white, Jewish, 18, sentenced for robbery, rape, inmate of reformatory.—Moving pictures are my delight. I always pictured myself as the Bad man. Boy, how I used to beat up the hero. I sure was tough. Cops I used to bump off by the squads. Of course, this was all imagination or daydreaming. After I would come out of a show I would call my bunch of boy friends and girls together. I was the leading bo at all times. I would pick out a guy that I did not like and say "you are the good guy." Then I would pick out the toughs for my side. As I always was the Big Shot, I used my right fist as a persuader and it never did fail me. I always was the bad guy and I would never lose.

One can see from the accounts that have been given that the witnessing of motion pictures may occasion phantasy of criminal behavior. The individual may project himself, imaginatively, into the rôle of a bold gangster, a clever bandit, a powerful gang leader, or similar characters. One cannot declare with certainty that phantasy or daydreaming of this sort induces one to crime. Yet it is not unreasonable to presume that it may, and perhaps does. The belief by some criminals that their criminal phantasies had something to do with their careers suggests the likelihood of a similar relation in the case of others, even though it may not be consciously observed by them. If the playing out of rôles in one's imagination be thought of as not only expressing certain impulses and desires, but also of organizing them and, perhaps, of stimulating them, it would seem reasonable that criminal phantasy should dispose one to crime. This does not mean that it causes one to commit crime. The presence of the daydreaming of criminal rôles in many people who never engage in crime would immediately falsify such an assertion. In their instances the checking of criminal temptations—perhaps even disinclination on their part to do anything criminal—nullifies any incitatory effects of their daydreams.[7] Yet in the experience of an individual who lives under social conditions where criminal activity has a quasi-reputability and acceptance, where the temptations to engage in crime are greater—as in many slum areas—it can be seen that imagining oneself as a gangster or bandit might lead the more easily to delinquency.

It is with this thought in mind that the discussion and cases in this section have been presented. The fact that the number of delinquents and criminals who speak of having imagined themselves in criminal rôles exceeds those who feel that movies have had something to do with their criminal acts suggests, in the light of our discussion, an indirect and undetected effect of the movies in their cases.

D. DISPLAY OF CRIME TECHNIQUES

Our material points to another indirect way in which movies of the conventional run may contribute to delinquency or crime. This is by picturing forms of criminal activity—ways of burglarizing, of robbing, of escaping detection, of avoiding pursuit, and of similar schemes. Many criminal ways of this sort may be seen in motion pictures and remembered, even though they may not be put to either immediate or eventual use. They exist in memory or in one's stock of images as latent implements, available for use if the occasion demands. In the previous chapter instances were given of the direct use by criminals and delinquents of crime techniques seen in motion pictures. Those which are used are fewer, considerably, than those which are learned.

Of the sample of 110 convicts whose experiences were studied with respect to the item under consideration, it

[7] This mechanism is illustrated in the account which appears on bottom of page 151.

was found, for example, that 20 per cent affirmed that motion pictures taught them ways of stealing. Twenty-one per cent of the same group stated that motion pictures taught them how to fool the police. This proportion exceeds, again, the number who have felt motion pictures to have contributed to their criminal acts or career. The difference suggests once more a latent or indirect influence by motion pictures.

In accordance with our general plan, let us present now a number of accounts, taken from the autobiographies of criminals, of techniques of crime witnessed by them in motion pictures.

Male, white, Jewish, 18, sentenced for robbery and rape, inmate of reformatory.—I have learned a lot from the movies as a burglar. One way of getting into a place is to get a job as gas inspector. Go to the door. If no one answers go around to the back door. Go through the transom or window, "prowl" the place and then leave.

Male, white, 23, sentenced for burglary, ex-convict.—I learned something in the ——————. It's a gangster picture. It shows how to drown out shots from a gun by backfiring a car.

Male, white, 30, robbery, ex-convict.—In a picture the rich girl was speeding and a motor cop caught up with her; she swung her car and killed the cop. If I ever was getting chased by a motor cop I'd think that would be a good way of ending the chase. That is just one of those fugitive ideas that I got from that one show.

Male, white, 23, sentenced for burglary, inmate of reformatory.—I have learned many ways about committing crime. There are many ways to commit a crime like murder and rape, highjacking, stick-ups, burglary, and assault. These are all stock crimes and all but one or two you can learn from a movie. There are many ways that you can learn at the movies of how to pull a job. You can have a place spotted out and take 4 or 5 fellows with you if you are robbing a bank. You can stop a block away from the bank and let them go on to the bank on foot and the driver of the car and the guard in the car follow them and park by the bank. One of the three stay out in front by the door and the others go in the bank and get the money that they came after, and then get in the car that is waiting for them and drive off. That is one way of pulling a job and fooling the police. This I have seen in the movies.

Male, white, 25, sentenced for burglary, ex-convict.—At one of the comedies I saw I got an idea how to remove iron bars in front of a window, quick and sure. It showed how a truck that was parked and some kids came up and tied a rope onto the truck to some iron bars. The driver came out and got into the truck and down the street, taking the bars with him, and continued doing a lot of crazy stunts that these kids would pull. But I thought if some one wanted to pull a jail break or to remove these bars it would be quick and sure. Of course, not that I have tried it, but there's a possibility in doing it, if you ever wanted to.

In another picture I saw how a guy used a rag saturated with ether and he put it on the face of a sleeping man, and went ahead and "prowled" the place. This is also an idea, and I know it could be used effectively.

In another picture I saw there were some burglars and all they were interested in was collecting the silverware. I thought of the thousands of dollars worth of stuff I had passed up in the homes I had ransacked.

Another thing I learned and I think it was from one of the pictures, is to wear gloves. They have my fingerprints now, and if it was a "big" case they would look for prints. By wearing gloves you wouldn't leave these little telltale prints.

I saw one picture where they had a plate in front of a safe and if you stepped on this plate it would snap your picture. Well this fellow was burning the safe and he stepped on the plate and that was the way they caught him. That was another idea I got. To be on the lookout for plates that would betray you by alarm or any other purpose of detection. And, also, that an "Arc" burner can be used to burn out the combination of a safe, without noise, and with less danger of detection and physical harm.

One can certainly get an education in a movie; that is, if his mind runs in that track.

List of Techniques of Crime.—A partial inventory of the techniques of crimes observed or learned from the motion pictures that appear in our materials includes:

How to open a safe by "feel" of dial.

How to enter store by forcing lock with crowbar and screw driver.

To cut burglar alarm wires of store to be burglarized in advance, during the day.

How to take door off hinges to force way into apartment for burglarizing it.

How to break window noiselessly for forcing entrance into store or house to be burglarized, by pasting flypaper on window before breaking it.

Technique of how to act and what to do in robbery with a gun.

Use of brace and bit to drill lock out for forcing entrance into store.

Use of glass cutter to cut glass of window away so window lock can be opened.

Technique of sudden approach and quick get-away in robbery.

How to jimmy a door or window.

Use a master key for gaining entrance to house.

Idea of looking for secret panels hiding wall safes in burglarizing house.

How to open or close lock with pair of tweezers.

How to force door on automobile with a piece of pipe.

Idea of stealing silverware in burglaries.

Idea of renting apartment for gang "hangout."

"Scientific way of pulling jobs. Leave no fingerprints or telltale marks."

"How to use weapons—pistols, shotguns, machine guns, black-jacks, brass knuckles, bombs."

Eluding police by turning up alley, turning automobile light off—waiting and then departing in the opposite direction.

Making money by gambling (and cheating) with drunken persons.

To pose as a gas inspector—ring doorbell and if someone answers inspect the gas. If no one is at home force way in and burglarize apartment.

How to drown out shots of guns by backfiring a car.

How to maim or kill motorcycle policeman chasing automobile by swinging and stopping car suddenly.

How to pick pockets.

How to accomplish jail breaks by using truck to pull bars from windows or door.

The use of ether on sleeping occupants of house being burglarized.

The use of gloves in burglary to prevent leaving fingerprints.

To beware of alarms or plates in front of safes that betray you.

The use of an "Arc-burner" to burn out combination of safe without noise.

How to sell liquor in "booze racket" by coercion.

Importance of establishing alibi.

Possible Use of Such Techniques.—These instances suggest some of the ways of crime which have been seen in watching motion pictures. We have already spoken of the obvious point that merely to see some clever form of crime in a picture does not mean that it will be followed. Certainly most movie-goers, including all age groups, would not utilize the technique shown. Neither, as the materials indicate, will it be taken up by all of those with distinct criminal tendencies. Many of this group may not be interested in the technique. Many may discount what is shown, regarding it as spectacular but of little practical value.[8] Actually, those who would be likely to make immediate use of the technique would be few—confined, essentially, to those who see in it a promise to the realization of some immediate interest of theirs. Notwithstanding this, it seems clear that some memory of what has been seen is likely to be retained by those who are interested. (The criminal, delinquent, or marginal individual is usually always interested in the portrayal of crime in motion pictures.) Memories of such crime techniques, as we have already said, always offer the possibility of being of service some time in the future. Perhaps an instance would help to make the point clear.

Male, Negro, 22, sentenced for burglary, inmate of reformatory.—I recall a time when we were trying to rob a flat on the south side of Chicago. We could not get the door open. I decided to give it up and try another one. One of the boys by the name of K—— said "I will show you how to open the door." He took the screw driver and took the strips off the back of the door. After he had completed that task, he took the hammer and the screw driver and knocked the bolts out of the hinges. Then we lifted up the door and went in and robbed the flat. When we got back to our neighborhood we went under the elevator tracks and split up the loot. When that was finished, K—— told us about the way he had shown us how to get into the flat we had just robbed, that he had seen a feller do it in a moving picture.

This case suggests how information about crime, secured from motion pictures, may be retained as a reservoir of knowledge that may be drawn upon as occasion demands.

[8] *Male, white, 24, sentenced for burglary, inmate of reformatory.*—Movies have never taught me to pull a job, open a safe or any other things concerning a criminal career, for the simple reason every good plot or way of pulling a job is usually foiled in the attempt or run down pretty quick in another way. I have never attempted to follow the movie way of doing things.

Male, white, 21, sentenced for burglary, inmate of reformatory.—Movies bring out ways of stealing and beating the law very plainly. I have seen lots of ways to open safes and so forth, but I have always thought they were faked.

Male, white, 19, sentenced for burglary, inmate of reformatory.—I have seen many things in pictures that have given me ideas about pulling jobs. I have never used them because many are too hard.

E. RELATION TO TRUANCY

Before concluding this discussion of the indirect ways [9] in which motion pictures may contribute to, or reënforce, criminal behavior we call attention to still one other—the promotion of truancy.

Seventeen per cent of the truant and behavior-problem boys, 6 per cent of the boys in the high-rate delinquency areas, 9 per cent of the boys in the medium-rate delinquency areas, and 7 per cent of the boys in the low-rate delinquency areas state that movies have made them want to run away from school. Four per cent of the truant and behavior-problem boys, 4 per cent of the school boys in the high-rate delinquency areas, 2 per cent of the boys in the medium-rate delinquency areas, and 1 per cent of the boys in the low-rate delinquency areas indicate that movies have made

[9] There seems to be a possible connection between the playing of criminal rôles in childhood play and subsequent criminal dispositions. The connection, however, has not been established. Some suggestions along this line appear in the following accounts:

Male, white, 24, sentenced for robbery, inmate of reformatory.—I liked to play Cowboy and Indians. It wasn't a bad game. I was always the Cowboy because I used a gun good. I practiced so much that I got to be fast with a gun. I believe it was born in me to use a gun. I always carried a gun from the age of ten. I had many a thrashing for showing off. I beat a cop drawing from the shoulder in Detroit and I beat a railroad policeman in Nashville, Tenn., and like a d——fool shot him in the hand.

Male, white, 23, sentenced for robbery, inmate of reformatory.—As soon as I got to be old enough to wander around a little without getting lost, my first thing I done was to get acquainted with the other neighborhood tots and we would all get our nickels together and go to see a thrilling western or crook picture that happened to be showing in the neighborhood. It was a great thrill to see the guns in action in a big train robbery or cattle rustling breakup. As soon as we got tired of looking straight up at pictures we would decide to go back to the neighborhood and start our evening game of "cops and robbers." It used to be hard for us kids to decide as to who would be the "coppers" because everyone wanted to be the bold robber they just saw in the moving pictures. As a small lad I did not have much use for a copper in crook plays, I always hoped the robber would get the best of the copper. I got a kind of grudge up when I saw the copper conquering the robber, I decided some day to grow up and show the coppers something, but I was only a child then. The boys always used to choose me for their chief robber, because I was the biggest and strongest, and if they wouldn't choose me as chief, I would punch a few of them and break up the game. I always was a very bad man for the kid coppers to catch and if they would corner me, I'd fight my way out. So, you see how much pictures were responsible in starting me up in the racket.

them want to run away from home. To the extent that it is true, as Rodney Brandon, Director of the Department of Public Welfare in the State of Illinois, recently pointed out, that the criminal is essentially a "schoolless, homeless, churchless, foot-loose individual," the influence of the motion pictures in helping to divorce the individual from his school and home becomes especially significant. The foot-loose boy who has run away from school and home finds substitute social institutions which transmit patterns of behavior to him, and these substitutes are frequently in the form of delinquent or criminal gangs. Some phases of this indirect influence of motion pictures on delinquency and crime will be treated more fully in the chapter on "Female Delinquency."

F. Summary

In this chapter we have been concerned with some indirect ways by which motion pictures may promote criminal tendencies or behavior. We have declared that by arousing desires for "easy money," by inducing a spirit of bravado, toughness, and adventurousness, by fostering the day-dreaming of criminal rôles, by displaying techniques of crime, and by contributing to truancy, motion pictures may lead or dispose to crime. We have spoken of these influences as indirect, because while they act directly on thoughts and feelings, many delinquents and criminals are not aware of them as linked up with their delinquent or criminal behavior. While this indirect connection is not proved conclusively, we have sought to show through the use of our materials that the presumption of such a connection is large. A summary statement should help to make the point clear.

We wish to call attention, first, to the fact that the number of delinquents and criminals who speak of being influenced by motion pictures in certain ways which we might think of as associated with crime, exceeds those who admit that motion pictures have actually contributed to their delinquency or crime. While approximately 10 per cent of the male delinquents and criminals studied feel that motion pictures contributed to their wrongdoing, larger proportions (of the sample of 110 criminals) speak of these specific influences. Thus: 49 per cent say that the movies give one the desire to carry a gun, 28 per cent declare that they give one the desire to practice stick-ups, 20 per cent that the movies have taught them ways of stealing, 21 per cent that movies taught them ways of fooling the police, 12 per cent that they had planned to hold up someone or "pull a job" when they saw an adventuresome bandit or gangster picture, 45 per cent that the movies suggest ways of getting money easily, 26 per cent that the movies led them to be daring and to act "tough," 20 per cent that certain movies led them to daydream of being a gangster or burglar.

There are two reflections which suggest that motion pictures in inducing such effects are likely to dispose to crime, even though many may not have observed particularly such a relation in their own experiences.

For one thing, these effects are of the sort that fit naturally into the pattern of crime, or, stated otherwise, they represent elements which are usually recognized as forming part of the general pattern of crime. Thus a wish to carry a gun and to practice a stick-up with it, an idea of stealing or of fooling the police, a planning of how to hold up someone, or to pull a job, desires of getting "easy money," a spirit of bravado or an inclination to act "tough," and imagining oneself as a gangster or burglar carrying out a criminal act—all these are traits of criminal behavior. It seems reasonable to infer that any agency like motion pictures which prompts people to such ideas, to such feelings, to such inclinations, and to such phantasy disposes them to delinquency or crime, making it easier for them to engage in crime.

That the truth of this presumption is likely is shown by the other observation—the recognition that there are always a few delinquents and criminals who can trace in their own experience a connection between such influences and their own crime. What presents itself as a conscious connection to some, may exist as an unconscious connection in the experience of others.

This is the interpretation made by the authors of the material presented in this chapter. The materials are given, so the readers may judge for themselves as to the reasonableness of the interpretation.

CHAPTER IV

MALE SEXUAL DELINQUENCY AND CRIME [1]

ONE of the most popular and recurrent motion picture themes is that centering around love and sex. In the preceding chapter, under the heading "Emotional Possession," brief attention was paid to the high emotional pitch to which boys and young men may be aroused by motion pictures. There we were concerned primarily with the feeling of adventurousness, daring, and "toughness." In investigating the effects of love pictures it becomes clear that motion pictures may also incite emotional possession of a sexual character. In doing so it may contribute to, or reënforce, the pattern of dispositions associated with sexual offenses. In this chapter [2] we are presenting autobiographical material from several convicts which indicate the manner in which passionate love pictures may be received. We are also giving, at a little greater length, a case of a young man, serving a sentence for attempted rape, in whose experience we may detect as one factor the influence of motion pictures.

Let us present first some questionnaire responses. Of a sample of 110 inmates of a penal institution 12 per cent stated that the movies stirred them sexually; 19 per cent indicated that an exciting picture makes them want to make love to a girl; while 35 per cent indicated that the movies have taught

[1] In the autobiographical accounts in this and the following chapter it has been found advisable to modify considerably the language, in the interests of publication. The accounts while frank in statement are not expressions of sexual boasting.
[2] The rôle of motion pictures in the sex delinquencies of girls is considered in the chapter on "Female Delinquency."

them how to attract girls, how to flirt, kiss, or make love.[3]

Some appreciation of the excitation of sexual impulses by certain kinds of motion pictures will be given by the autobiographical accounts which follow.

White, Italian, 16, high-rate delinquency area.—I didn't care for love pictures, and I don't like them. I'd rather see a funny picture or "hot" pictures for adults only. I like to sit next a girl when they'd show them. I'd get sexually aroused. Once in a while I'd take a girl to a show to get her warmed up but after the show I couldn't get very far. It was the same old thing, leaving her at home. When I saw —————— in ——————, she went in the water, and her bathing suit came off. The girl was warmed up and so was I, and I started to play around. I got pretty far.

White, Italian, 16, high-rate delinquency area.—I like some love pictures, like —————— plays in. When you see these hot love pictures it makes you feel like going out and having sexual relations. A guy was out in a garden with a girl and after he became a father he left the girl. Pictures like that make a guy feel like going out and doing things. I took a girl to one of these pictures and we followed the picture and did everything they did in the picture. I got what I was after later.

White, Polish, 23, burglary, inmate of state reformatory.—I would go to a sex picture but I always have a girl with me. Whenever I would see the lover on the screen begin making love to the heroine, I would put one arm around my girl (we always sat in the back of the theater so that nobody would be around us), and with the other hand I would make many advances to her. She'd begin to get aroused and if it happened to be during the early part of the afternoon and not many people within the show I would have sexual relations with her on the floor between the last two rows of seats.

Later on I got invited to parties and did we have hot times? We'd begin by discussing the different sex pictures we had seen

[3] For further data on this point see in *Movies and Conduct:* the chapters on "Emotional Possession"; "Love and Passion"; and "Imitation by Adolescents."

and the manner in which the hero made love to the girl. It would finally end up with a girl in each boy's lap, kissing and playing with each other; and finally each boy would take his girl.

The arousal of sex passion by motion pictures does not necessarily lead, of course, to sexual misconduct. That it may play a part in doing so, however, is pointed to by the accounts of experiences we have given, and is made even clearer in the additional accounts which follow.

White, 22, sentenced for robbery, inmate of reformatory.—The sex pictures are ones a lot of us go to, just to get excited. Afterwards we go to a house of prostitution and satisfy our desires.

Negro, 22, sentenced for burglary, inmate of reformatory.—I went to a sex picture when I was thirteen and when I came out I had a funny feeling all over. I met a girl 16 years old whom I knew and she said "Did you just come out of the show?" I said yes. She took me to her room and took care of me all night. We were in the same bed. That was my first dealing with females. After that I always went to sex pictures and to parties.

White, Polish, 23, sentenced for burglary, inmate of reformatory.—I have seen lots of love and sex pictures and I enjoyed watching all of them. After watching these pictures I would always feel hot and passionate all over. I would especially watch how the lover would kiss the girl and how his hands would stray all over her glorious body. I would have a strange, delightful feeling and get very aroused. After leaving the show I would go back to the neighborhood and start talking to the gang about the picture and my subsequent reaction to it. We would all get together and discuss various ways and means of getting a girl to come down to our hangout (which was situated in an old abandoned quarry) and then hold a "tete a tete" with her.

The writer of this account continues with a description of their success in enticing a girl into their quarters and then raping her.

The following case is presented in some detail because it reveals over a period of time the influence of the pictures on the sexual behavior of the writer. This document was written by an ex-convict who served a sentence for rape, an offense in which motion pictures played a prominent part. He begins his narrative with a brief résumé of his early childhood, tells how he became a member of a boys' gang, and describes their various activities.

> *White, 23, sentenced for rape, ex-convict.*—One night we went up to the ——— (a motion picture theater) but couldn't get our regular seats. I got one right near to a broad I went to school with and she was a keen kid in school and never fooled around much. So I just sat there and talked with her and watched the picture. ————— was playing in a serial at that time, and she was a pretty clever actress. It was a good show. After the show was over we went outside and I went walking with ———. We walked around for about a half hour and then went up to her house and sat on her front steps just talking. Gee, I don't know, but I just couldn't figure it out. This kid falling for me; she had looks—decent girl—and everything. I went home that night promising her I would meet her the next night at the show. The next night I did meet her; and gosh! I am acting and sounding goofy now, but I guess I was falling hard. We went home that night too without anything happening. I met the bunch on the corner after I left her and they started to razz me and said she was pretty desirable and tried to fix it for me to walk her over around the beach the next night.
>
> I refused to do so, telling them that she was a good, clean, respectable girl; and T—— laughed and said, "Boy, she's had plenty of sex relations." I was a good fighter, but I was mad, and for winning a fight I was second best that night as far as fighting was concerned. But I was hot and didn't give a damn. I picked up a house brick and started to run and threw it at him and hit him in the back of the head, and he fell unconscious.

It is clear from the above narration that the writer was in love with the girl he was escorting to the movies and was convinced at the time that she was a "good, clean, respectable girl." In fact, the challenge of her respectability invoked him to a quarrel and fight which resulted in the severance of his relations with his gang. He continued to go to the movies with the girl, as described below:

About a week or so after the fight with T——, I met M—— again and we went up to a show. I started to put my arm around her and kiss her and she didn't move. Now, I know she was only a "little bum," but at that time I thought she was in love with me. A new life opened up to me that night. I was all "bubbles." I played around, contented in just kissing and loving her. We didn't go to the shows much then. We wanted to be alone; and this went on for a couple of nights or so. I would meet her at about six-thirty or seven and bum around until eleven or twelve o'clock.

We went to the show Sunday afternoon down at T—— Street and M——, and it was a raw picture—"Adults Only," and we got in. The part of the picture that aroused me and her too, I guess, was when the guy was loving up the woman on a couch and she leaned back and he got over her and was kissing her and loving her. M—— had ahold of my hand, and her hand was all wet with sweat, and she said, "J——, that is the way I would like to have you love me." I looked at her and she looked into my eyes and looked as if she was going to faint. We did not wait for all the show, but left.

After we got outside, she acted different. I was stirred up in the show but cooled off after we walked a block or so. It was about five P.M. when we got over to M——'s house, and I told her I would meet her after supper. I went home and had supper. Then I went over there and whistled for M——. She came to the door and told me to come up. I was never in her house before and I went up. Her mother had gone to visit somebody and no one was home. We went in the front room and sat down; and after we sat down and kissed a while she wanted to be loved like the girl in the picture, and I done exactly that.

I got all stirred up, but, at first couldn't ask her for sexual relations. I didn't have the nerve, I guess. She was aroused too and showed it plenty. Finally after fooling around for about a half hour like this, we had sexual relations.

Although, as is revealed in the document elsewhere, both had had sexual experiences prior to the above incident, it is important to note that the character of their relationship, to begin with, was essentially a typical adolescent love affair. Undoubtedly their earlier experiences in part explain their receptivity, but it is significant that the motion pictures aroused sex passion in both of them and suggested techniques of love-making which helped to lead up to sex relations.

In continuing his narrative the writer tells us how he secured a position with a reputable business organization and became successful as a salesman. In the central offices of his firm he met a young girl of sixteen who attracted him very much. He keeps company with her for several weeks, is introduced to her mother, and his attitude towards the girl is evident from his remark, "Boy, I'd have married her right then and there if she'd asked me." Up to this point he is clearly in love with the girl in a socially acceptable manner, but his sex passion becomes inflamed to a point where he determines to have sexual relations with her.

> Sunday afternoon I made up my mind I was going to have intercourse with her, if I had to force it. How to get her aroused was the next thing. I read the picture part of the paper, and ———— ———————— was playing. I took B——, and that picture was the "hit." It was really sizzling in parts. B——'s got "it"; and you know if you ever wanted to have intercourse with a girl all you got to do is to take her to one of those plays. They give her the idea. She gets aroused, and the next is up to you. B—— was aroused. I know that because I made many preliminary advances to her during the show, and she did not resist. After the show we went to ———— and had chop suey. Next we went to —— Street and —— Street (an isolated section of the city) and stopped.
>
> Well, she petted and became aroused again. I was sure from her reactions and the nature of my advances to which she did

not object that she was ready for relations, but when I tried it she screamed and started to cry. I tried to use force, but she resisted. I let her go and tried to patch things up, but she wouldn't talk. I drove her home.

The next morning when I showed up for work, the girl, her family, my bosses, and a policeman met me.

The narrator was convicted for attempted rape as a result of the above incident and served a sentence of three years. The above case indicates not only that the motion pictures may excite passions that may lead to sexual relations but also that observers may become aware of this influence and consciously use the motion pictures for arousing the desires of their girl companions as a preliminary to further advances.

The discussion in this chapter indicates that in the experience of some boys and young men, passionate love pictures may be a sexual excitant. In many cases, motion pictures may also furnish observers love techniques that facilitate the expression of their aroused desires. This stirring up of sexual passion need not lead to sexual misconduct but that it may do so is clear. The sexual delinquencies which result may be comparatively mild, as in illicit sexual relations with the consent of the girl, or they may work into more serious forms, as in the case of rape by the individual or a gang. Of some significance is the observation that male observers may become aware of the power of passionate love pictures and use them as a means of arousing girls to the desired pitch of excitement and passion.[4]

[4] For influence of motion pictures on sexual behavior see also in Chapter V: "Female Delinquency and Crime," the sections on "Emotional Possession" and "Imitation and Sex Delinquency"; and in Chapter VIII: "Motion Pictures in Correctional and Penal Institutions," the section on "Discipline Value of Motion Pictures" dealing with the effects of love pictures shown in the institutions.

CHAPTER V

FEMALE DELINQUENCY[1]

LET us turn now to a consideration of the rôle of motion pictures in the delinquent behavior of girls and young women. Formerly the relatively sheltered life and restricted range of contacts of women as compared with men made female delinquency or crime comparatively rare. In modern times, however, as we might expect from the changing rôle of woman with her unceasing participation in areas of life previously closed to her, female delinquency and crime are on the increase. The delinquency of girls and young women is still confined chiefly to sexual misdemeanors. Consequently, although we will make some reference to non-sexual forms of delinquency, our materials deal largely with sex misbehavior.

Motion pictures may be regarded as one element in the new world of experience recently opened to women. Through visual presentation they have made vivid forms of life and kinds of experiences which previously were outside their observation and which were conceived, at best, merely in imagination. This display of fascinating life and experience coveted by many girls and young women has been influential, as we shall see, in leading to delinquency.

We may begin our discussion by mentioning that of a group of 117 delinquent girls in a state training school, 25 per cent indicated that the movies were a direct contribut-

[1] This chapter is based on materials gathered from girls who are mainly sexual delinquents, truants, and runaways. Therefore, its findings and interpretations pertain to these types of delinquents.

ing influence to their own delinquency.   This is probably a conservative figure because of the possibility of indirect or undetected influence in the case of others.   As we shall see, the number of delinquents who acknowledge receiving from motion pictures specific effects which are ordinarily associated with delinquency exceeds considerably the 25 per cent who admit the influence of motion pictures on their delinquency.

Our treatment will follow the plan of considering the chief ways in which motion pictures seem to lead some, and dispose others, to delinquency.

A. SEXUAL PASSION AND DELINQUENCY [2]

One of the chief ways by which motion pictures seem, unwittingly, to encourage delinquency in the case of some girls and young women is in arousing sex passion.[3] In the case of many of the sexually delinquent girls studied, the autobiographical evidence shows in an impressive way how passionate love pictures may act as a sexual excitant.   In witnessing such pictures many of these girls have experienced strong sex desires—sometimes almost of a compulsive character—which made them markedly receptive to advances by men.   A series of autobiographical accounts will illustrate how passions may be aroused.

White, 17, sexual delinquent.—I am a girl interested in a good Passionate Love Picture.   What a grand and glorious thrill a good love picture awakens in me.   The first love picture I went to with a boy was ——————————.   I sure got a thrill.   When you see a real love picture you feel more like being loved than before. . . . Things like that makes you feel funny

[2] See footnote 1 on page 73.
[3] Some consideration of the influence of passionate love pictures on adolescents is given in the author's companion report on *Movies and Conduct* in the chapter "Emotional Possession: Love and Passion."

especially when you are with your lover and he loves you. You have a funny sensation down in your heart. When I see a picture that has love in it, it makes me jealous. Why? Because I want loving too. Sometimes when there is a love picture of a boy and girl I feel like going up there and telling her to let me love a while.

White, 16, sexual delinquent.—Gosh! when I see a good-looking fast fellow I get all excited. If I only had a chance like those in the movies I'd have a good time because when I see a fellow and a girl in a passionate love scene, such as in the —————— love scene, I just have a *hot* feeling going through me and I want to do everything bad. When a girl really loves a fellow and he takes her to his house and makes her stay there with him, she gives in to his wants like in the ——————. —————— played in it. He took her in his arms and bent her backward and kissed her and went through all kinds of thrilly motions that make us kids get all flustrated. Oh! for a life in the movies with a vagabond lover.

White, 16, sexual delinquent.—The first movie that I ever remember seeing before I was 14 years old was the picture ——————. I couldn't hardly sit in my seat when I saw this young girl and boy sitting under a tree expressing their love and congratulations to each other; especially when their eyes would meet, they would sure charm me. . . . The movies that excite me and make me fall into my lover's arms are passionate or love plays. They give you just what you are craving for: *Love.*

White, 17, sexual delinquent.—Wanting to do things that were exciting and unlawful was the main thing that brought me up here (*i.e.*, to the state training school). The movies played a most important part in my life. Going to the movies with girl-friends and boy-friends and getting stirred up sexually was one of the things I most desired.

White, 14, truant, runaway.—After I come home from seeing a picture, I mean a romantic love picture, oh I feel all excited as usual. When I do see a romantic love picture like that I can't wait till I get old enough to do things like that. Of course, I'm young now, only a kid. Of course, I go out with fellows 24 or 25 who have brains and the dough.

White, 14, truant, runaway.—Well, here goes: The sort of movie I like best is Love; in other words you can say Romance. One film I liked best was Rudolph Valentino in "The Sheik." It was the most romantic and lovable picture I have ever seen. It taught me to crave a lover like Rudy; he kisses his partner wonderfully. I often say to myself I wish I was the woman in the play. Every time I heard of a play that Valentino played in I begged mother to let me go. I wasn't in my teens yet either. Ever since a little child I craved love movies. . . . After I've seen a romantic love scene I feel as though I couldn't have just one fellow to love me, but I would like about five; and on the way home I have a feeling or desire to have a fellow kissing me all the time or I mean a different fellow to kiss me every minute of the day. But when I see a romantic love scene and I am with a fellow, I like to have him put his arm around me and hold my hand and keep his head close to mine; in other words, I mean his cheek. When I'm watching the play I'm so dreamy that I could fall asleep in the fellow's arms, and another thing when I'm sitting there so interested in the movie and then when the fellow slips his arm about me, it gives me sort of a thrill just like a chill going down my back. And after we leave the theater, I mean the boy-friend and I, well of course, he takes me home and, well, the part I like most is when *we* are sitting on the sofa and he makes believe that he is a lover like Rudy Valentino and of course I'm so thrilled I really don't know what to do. First, he kisses my forehead, then my cheeks, and then my lips and his lips are so feverish that they hold me spellbound. Sometimes I don't know what to think of him, he acts so restless.

Of a sample of 252 delinquent girls in a state training school, 121, or 48 per cent, acknowledge that they usually "felt like having a man make love to them" after they had seen a passionate love picture; 118, or 47 per cent, declared that they did not have this experience; while 13, or 5 per cent, were non-committal.

These statistical data and the accounts cited point to the way in which certain types of motion pictures may work upon the careers of some girls. In these cases the distance between feelings of passionate love and sexual behavior is small. While the passionate feelings which are aroused may express themselves solely in the field of imagination or in kissing and caressing, frequently, as our materials indicate, they may prompt the girl to engage in sex relations.

Negro, 18, sexual delinquent.—Of course I was warned against men, but still like all other girls I didn't take any heed of what they told me. So I just went around like other girls with men until I got into trouble. The movie that appealed to me was Vilma Banky in "The Sheik." Of course that movie thrilled me a great deal. Other pictures with men making love to women, I guess, were the cause of me "fooling" with men.

White, 17, sexual delinquent.—About the movies—my mother always did like them and she would take me up town and my dad would rave. Then when I started running around he said it was account of "movies." Well, maybe movies did have something to do with it. Anyway, when I'd see in the movies "petting parties," smoking and liquor, I naturally got the desire to indulge in them and I did. Of course, after seeing a good-looking blond man, I get the desire to get with one, and I did. Hence, all the trouble.

White, 17, sexual delinquent.—I always went to shows that were for adults only. I can truthfully say that I understood almost all of the pictures I saw and that the more I saw them the more I wanted to see them. I can't say that they were to blame for my being here, but they played an important part in my sexual life.

White, 16, sexual delinquent.—When I was on the outside I went to the movies almost every night, but only about twice in two months to a dance. I didn't like dances as well as I do movies. A movie would get me so passionate after it was over that I just had to have satisfaction. You know what I mean. If you don't I tell you in plain English and that is, to have sexual relations.

White, 16, sexual delinquent.—Passionate love pictures make me think most. I wish when I see the fellow and the girl play the part that I was the girl in place of the one in the picture. It makes me think of going out with a good passionate man or going to a place and having a good old hot time, as we call it. It makes me feel the thrill of how I would want to be loved. I think I got some of my actions from love scenes. It taught me how to act in the presence of the fellow I love. It makes me think of strolling in the moonlight with some good-looking fellow. And to be with him alone. . . . When I see movies that excite me I always want to go home and do the same things that I saw them do. Pictures where a fellow kisses a girl and holds her a long time is what gets me excited, and I just want to do that myself. . . . Passionate love pictures do stir me up. Some and most times I go out from a movie and stay out late with a fellow. Sometimes never think of coming in till 2:30 in the morning. . . . One night I went to a movie with a fellow of mine, who drove a very chic little sport roadster. In the movie he sat with his arms around me, and every time the fellow would kiss the girl he would look at me lovingly and squeeze my hand; after the movie we went to my girl friend's house and got her and her fellow. Then we all four went for a moonlight spooning ride, and had sexual relations.

White, 17, sexual delinquent.—I like to see men and women fall in love in the movies and go out on parties, etc. It teaches me how to do the same. I also like to see them kiss, love, drink, smoke, and lead up to sex relations. It makes me get all stirred up in a passionate way. Love pictures, Wild West pictures, murder cases are the pictures I like best, because I like to love, myself, and I know others want to do the same. After I see them I go out and love and have sexual relations and go on parties and only do worse. Movies teach me how to treat my men and fool them. When I see a Wild West picture, especially when I see a cowboy falling in love with a girl and running away with her and when they go out riding with her it makes me want to be out in the West—Colorado—with some one I could love around and have sexual relations with. When I saw the picture, "All Quiet on the Western Front," I was so thrilled and excited I could hardly realize I was seeing the picture. It seems as though it was myself and the boy I was sitting with. I have always wanted to have the experience and thrill of being held in the arms of some masculine man and being loved. . . . Love pictures are my favorites. They teach me how to love and kiss. Oh! ooooh! How thrilled I am when I see a real passionate movie! I watch every little detail, of how she's dressed, and her make-up, and also her hair. They are my favorite pictures. The most exciting pictures are passionate plays. I get excited most when they are kissing and loving and having experiences I wish I could have. When I see these movies I leave the movies most always immediately and go out to some roadhouse or an apartment with my man and have relations. Especially when I get all stirred up and my passion rises. I feel as if I never want my man to leave me, as if I can't live without him. I have a feeling that can't be expressed with words but with actions.

It is interesting to note that of the sample of 252 delinquent girls (most of them 14 to 18 years of age) 39 per cent acknowledge that they permitted men to make love or "pet" them after seeing passionate love pictures. Fifty-six per cent indicated this was not true in their case; 5 per cent did not respond to the question. Perhaps more significant is the finding that 25 per cent of the same sample acknowledged engaging in sexual relations after becoming sexually aroused at a movie. Sixty-nine per cent declared that this was not true in their experience. Six per cent did not respond to the question.

With few exceptions the girls from whom material was secured were in a state training school on charged of sexual delinquency. That they represent, consequently, a group peculiarly disposed to sexual experience is quite likely. Nevertheless, it seems quite clear that motion pictures were a direct contributing influence to the sexual propensity of many; and, it seems not unreasonable to infer, were an unnoticed influence in the case of others.

B. "FAST LIFE"

Closely allied to the arousing of love and sex passions, and yet more inclusive in so far as it involves a scheme of life, is the influence of motion pictures in creating desires for "fast life," "good times," "freedom," and "popularity." In contrast to their own life, which may appear to many of the girls as drab and colorless, pictures which portray a gay, fast life of wild parties and of attendance at cabarets and roadhouses seem to have a very strong appeal. Some idea of how such pictures may stimulate desires of enjoying a similar type of life and of evoking "wild" actions can be gained from the following accounts.

White, 16, sex delinquent.—The movies that get me exited most are those of high life, fighting, and love. What I mean by high life is a life of gambling, drinking, etc. When there is a love scene I anxiously await hoping to see the time come and wishing I were there when he takes her in his arms and bestows passionate kisses upon her. After I see a movie that excites me I'm ready for a good time. I go home with a longing to join the movies only if I could.

White, 15, truant, runaway.—The movies make me want to have a good time, but what kind of a good time is the question. Well! I like to go out with a fellow to a cabaret or to a lively dance. All I crave is excitement. I like to go to cabarets with a nice fellow who likes excitement. Also, I like to get up and sing a song or two; in other words I crave popularity and gayety. I like to be in with a noisy crowd so that when we go out we can have a "hell of a good time." I got much of this feeling from the picture in which ————— played. I can't recall the name of the play, but it was like this: her parents didn't approve of her going with this certain crowd, and she liked this crowd very much. She said she wouldn't stop going with this crowd because whenever she went out with them she had a "hell of a time." I'm using the correct words she used. I would feel the same way about it if my mother and dad disapproved of my company;

if there was anything wrong with them, I wouldn't care but if there wasn't I wouldn't break up with that crowd. Another play I saw was ———————— in ———————— and a week afterwards I went to a party; of course I mingled with the drinks as she had done. I also sang the theme song of ————————. That play made me want to be and act like those girls, and it gave me an idea about the modern girls of to-day.

White, 17, sexual delinquent.—When I saw ———————— in ————————, I craved nothing but love and a wild party. When I saw ———————— I wanted to try taking my sis' boy friend and finally I succeeded.

White, 14, truant, runaway.—The picture that made me feel good was ————————. It was about ———————— working in a restaurant singing, enjoying herself. I've tried to do the same thing but I was too bashful to get in front of a customer, a stranger, and sing like she did. Of course I would if I were a little peppier and hotter and bothered like she was.

White, 15, sexual delinquent.—I think that running around with the men is responsible for me getting into trouble. Going to love pictures and the desire for popularity is partly what got me up here today.

Forty-nine per cent of the sample of 252 girls state that the movies made them want to live a gay fast life; 49 per cent indicate they did not have this experience; while 2 per cent did not respond to the question. Forty-one per cent of the girls in the same sample declared that the motion pictures made them want to go to wild parties, cabarets, and roadhouses; while 56 per cent indicate no such influence and 3 per cent did not reply to the question.

To have these desires for a fast life or for wild parties as a result of seeing motion pictures does not necessarily lead to delinquent behavior. Some patterns of "wild life" depicted on the screen which are imitated by girls need not be regarded as delinquent. But the effort to follow these patterns may bring the girl into conflict with her parents and her school authorities. This may lead, in turn, to truancy, running away from home, and eventually to more serious delinquency. Forty-one per cent of the 252 inmates studied admitted that going to wild parties, cabarets, road-houses, etc., "like they do in the movies," got them "into trouble." [4]

In the following cases, some of which are given in detail, one can see how motion pictures may present an alluring life which may make a girl dissatisfied with her own life, and bring her into conflict with her parents or school authorities; and how this, in turn, may lead to truancy and to adventures of a questionable nature.

White, 15, truant, runaway.— ——————— was my idol. I wanted to be like her more than anything else. I wanted to be wild and to dance and sing and smoke and drink like she did but I was only 12 years old and that was out of the question because the boys I went out with were only about 16 and they didn't do those things, so I had to satisfy myself by just going to the movies and watching other people do those things. As I became older I started to go with older boys. I went to the movies at an average of five times in one week. . . . Then I became dissatisfied with home, and my girl friend and I planned running away. We thought we were all too old for the other girls the same age as us. So one day we ditched school and made up our mind to go away from home. Neither of us had any money.

So we started walking down S—— Street toward W—— Avenue. We were passing —— High School and I knew a lot of fellows that went to that school; so I met this one fellow I used to go with and had him take me to — St. and W—— to the C—— Highway. One of my girl friends worked at the corner of — St. and W—— at the T—— Inn. So I went in and got five dollars from her and told her where we were going. We started down the Highway and got as far as —— that night about eight o'clock. We went into a hotel and got a room for a dollar seventy-five. I'm writing this experience because it's

---

[4] This question, unfortunately, is somewhat ambiguous. The statistical results are given, subject to the reader's interpretation.

part of my life's history in movies and what effect they had on me. We met a couple of fellows that night and went and got beer. H——, that's my girl friend, got drunk from putting ashes in her beer. The fellows said they would call for us in the morning and we'd go out. Well, we got up before they came and checked out of the hotel. We got to the highway and started getting lifts and planned to get to ——————, and from there go to ——————. H—— played the drums in an orchestra so we were going to ———— to get a job in the orchestra. We knew the radio announcer there and he was going to get her a job. On our way from ———— we got a lift from a big moving van. We slept in the back of the truck and had the blankets over us. We got in ———————— and started out on Route 31 and after two days got in ——————. We had $3.00 left when we got there and we went to a show. We saw Moran and Mack in "The Two Black Crows." That wasn't very hot, but we went up to the rest-room and she slept. We got up to the radio station all right but there was a different radio announcer there and it had been announced over the radio about us and our description so the radio announcer sent a telegram to our parents and they sent one back saying H——'s brother would come for us in a car. That night we stayed at the radio announcer's apartment with him and his wife. Then the next day we had to go to the jail and stay there two nights. Her brother came for us and we went back to Chicago. So one day we had to go to the principal at L—— High School and he said he was going to put us away in a home. We ran out of his office and got on the nearest street car and went downtown and stayed down there all day. At night we went to the nearest highway and started getting lifts. I had such a cold I couldn't hardly talk. We met two fellows in a Ford sedan and they said they would get something for my cold. So we went to a roadhouse and they got a bottle for me. I had to drink a half a pint of moon for my cold. So we went up to the fellow's house. His parents had been out in California, so we stayed at his house all night. The fellows didn't harm me in any way because my girl friend took care that they didn't while I was in that condition. All went well that night but the next day we went back to Chicago. We ditched the boys. And we didn't have any money to buy anything to eat so my brother was having a party that night so I thought I'd go home. I went home and promised to behave and not ditch school again. I kept away from H—— for three months; then we started going together again and started ditching school again. I kept up ditching school until they brought me up for court trial. That day they sent me from court to the juvenile and I stayed there two nights. Then I got home again and went out every night—waiting for my trial to come up again. It came up the next Thursday, and I was put in the —— (school for truant and behavior problem girls). But I can't help thinking that movies was the ruination of me because that's where I got all my ideas. I admit I still like them, knowing that. But I think they are a lot of trash, and if I got out of here and went to a movie I would take it sensibly and not get all excited and not let those kinds of things get into my head again. I know I am different than these girls here, but I have to make the best of it. So I am one girl that has been injured by the movies.

White, 15, truant, runaway.—One love picture I saw was —— —— in ————————. She didn't look like anything like to-day, but still in all the picture was rather good. The next picture I saw was a play with ———— and ———— ——, about Paris. I liked this picture. There was plenty of love and plenty of fun. I seemed to care a lot about this picture, so I kept on going out to shows quite often. Once I saw a picture about ———— in ————. In this picture she flirted a lot and made whoopee with every boy. . . . I loved this picture and would love to see another one like that. I wish I could. Then I saw a picture with ———— in ————. I liked this picture because there was a lot of love in it. . . . Then I saw a picture, ————, with ————. This was another pretty picture of her flirting. In this picture she was first a cloak clerk in a dance hall; then she was a model, and I wanted to be a model, too, although I knew I never could be one. Then a little later I saw a pretty picture with ————. She really was pretty and she knew how to make love. She was full of pep. Then I quit school for one whole year and went to work. I was only 13 then. . . . One time we went out riding. We started quarreling. He said, This night I am going to take you back home. I answered, You will not. So we kept that up. That evening this Dago said, All right, I will leave you alone, but be ready to go home. So that day I and my girl friend moved from that apartment to another apartment. That evening I went out riding with another boy friend. . . . I kept on going out but I didn't pay any attention to school. I grew still wilder. One time we went out to a show. I saw a pretty picture, ————, with ————————. We had a pretty time after the show. We went out to a beer joint and the feller I had was a fish so I kept on asking him to buy me some more drinks, although I didn't drink mine. I kept on ordering beer, wine, and high balls. I drank the high balls, but not anything else. . . . The movies really do make me want to have a good time; and as far as I can see, I believe I do have my good times. . . . The movies some-times did make me feel discontented. They have given me one idea and that is of how much freedom I ought to have.

White, 17, sexual delinquent.—In some ways movies did make me dissatisfied with my own home. My father was a man who let me have my own way a good deal in everything *except* the company I chose to run with. He did not care how many girl friends I had, but even when I reached the age of sixteen he thought I was entirely too young to keep company with boys. You can see then how I felt when I saw pictures where girls lived together in small apartments and were their own boss. Oh, how I wanted to be in their position. I think, however, this was the only thing that made me dissatisfied with my home life.

White, 14, truant, runaway.—Movies sure do make me want to have good times—movies like ———————————— which ———————— and ———————— played in, also the juvenile star ——————. Movies also do make me long for nice cloth-ing—clothing like ———————— or a few others wear when they play. I thought one day as I was at the show seeing a good picture, if any of the movie stars want to come home late their parents allow them. Why shouldn't mine? So I started coming home at 3 or 6 in the morning and soon I landed in the Ju-venile Court, which I thought was a very bad place, of course, for a girl of my age to be. I got out within a month. It didn't do me no good. I started over again.

As a follow-up question to that which asked if motion pictures had aroused desires for "wild parties," etc., was that which inquired whether going to "wild parties," cabarets, and roadhouses "like they do in the movies," led the girls to stay away from school or to run away from home.

Thirty-eight per cent of the 252 girls studied declared that going to wild parties, cabarets, roadhouses, etc., led them to stay away from school. Fifty-seven per cent declared this not to be true in their case. Five per cent did not reply to the question. Thirty-three per cent of the girls indicated that a similar influence led them to run away from home, while 62 per cent did not acknowledge this to be the case and 5 per cent did not respond to the question.

According to these figures, then, over one third of the girls studied, 38 per cent, have been led through a desire for a gay, "fast life," such as is shown in motion pictures, to stay away from school; and slightly less, exactly one third, or 33 per cent, have been led through the same desire to run away from home.

These acts—truancy and running away from home—are delinquent acts in themselves but are of even greater significance in so far as they may lead to more serious forms of delinquency. The girl detached from family and school is especially amenable to the influences of agencies which may lead her to more serious forms of delinquency.

The desire to lead a gay, fast, wild life may lead not only to truancy and running away from home and thus indirectly to sexual delinquency but may also directly result in sex misconduct. In fact, the wild patterns of life as taken over by girls from the screen frequently include unrestrained conduct. "Having a good time" in the cabaret, roadhouse, or "wild party" setting is conducive to the letting down of conventional restraints. Added to aroused sex passion it may lead some to illicit sexual behavior.

White, 16, sexual delinquent.—We always went to a movie that was nothing but a real *passionate* picture; when we got out of the movie we all went for a *whoopee ride* or to some *wild parties.* We stayed out *all night* and in the morning we would end up in a *road house.* We used to *spend weeks and months like that.* My best times have not gone by yet. When I go back to Chicago again, I'll only go back to those happy days I used to know. I *fully understand* what a *passionate* scene can do to one who has led a *low* life. Those were my happiest days. But oh! that is *only a piece* of *MY PAST.*

White, 17, sexual delinquent.—The most responsible thing for getting me in trouble is these love pictures. When I saw a love picture at night and if I had to go home alone I would try and flirt with some men on the corner. If it was the right kind of a bad man he would take me to a dance or a wild party; at these parties I would meet other men that would be crazy for fast life. These are the kind of men that got me in trouble. I went with some boys that would tell me they would take me to a party or a dance and at the end it would end up at a lonely road or woods. Those are the kind of boys that led my life astray. Some boys I went with would kick me out of the car and tell me to walk home if I wouldn't give them what they wanted. The best thing I like is wild parties. Movies were the first thing that made me go astray.

White, 17, sexual delinquent.—I think the ones that are the most responsible for me being here are the love pictures. Drinking, men, and a desire for a good time. It seemed that after I saw the movies, and their endings, I felt as if I could do the same thing and get by. Of course, I don't think the movies really got me into trouble. But of course they did make me want to try different things I saw, dress like some of the actors, drink, and have what they call a good time and get by with it.

White, 18, sexual delinquent.—When you see a fast picture of life or a passionate picture then you get the desire to go to a party and go out all the more with men. Then men lead you on to drinking and smoking and we girls are foolish enough to consent to their love affair which means just another girl to most men.

White, 15, sexual delinquent.—The movies I have seen have not been altogether wild pictures but most of them that I have seen I wanted to take after, such as flirting and running around with men and other things. Some movies have been very valuable to me. I always like ————— and —————————. I just got a chance to see a little of ————— and after I saw that I wanted to run wild like she did. I already was in a home, but I disobeyed orders and the wishes of my parents and superiors and ran around nights after school. After ————— I ran around wild and came up here.

Negro, 19, sexual delinquent.—Well, the movies taught me how to live that "fast life." And how to go on wild parties with men. How to long for clothes and good times. It just made me want to lead the life that I saw in some of the movies. Fast life and easy money. The movies also teach one how to be popular.

In our questionnaire material it is found that of the 252 delinquent girls to whom was submitted the question, "Did going to wild parties, cabarets, roadhouses, etc., like they do in the movies, ever lead you to sexual delinquencies?" [5] 23 per cent replied in the affirmative, 61 per cent in the negative, and 16 per cent failed to reply. These figures give a general idea of how the display of forms of gay and unrestrained life in motion pictures may nurture desires and encourage conduct that may eventuate in delinquency.

C. DESIRE FOR LUXURY AND SMART APPEARANCE

We have noted the influence of the motion pictures in instilling desires for clothes, automobiles, wealth, and ease in boys and young men and in suggesting the idea of easily attaining them. Among girls and young women this influence of the movies seems even more pronounced, for a greater premium seems to be placed on fine clothes, appear-

---

[5] The question is somewhat ambiguous, but the replies are given for whatever they are worth.

ance, and a life of ease in the case of women. The girl who witnesses smart fashionable gowns in settings of splendor and luxury may find in them, in contrast to her own often cheap, flimsy, and outmoded apparel and drab routine existence, an irresistible appeal. In many cases the desire for luxury expresses itself in a smarter and more fashionable selection of clothes, house furnishings, etc., within the financial means of the girl; but, on the other hand, many of the girls and young women studied grow dissatisfied with their own clothes and manner of living and in their efforts to achieve motion picture standards frequently get into trouble.

Let us turn first to an examination of the nature of the desire for a life of luxury and ease.

Negro, 16, sexual delinquent.—In seeing movies you get a desire to have pretty clothes, automobiles, and several other things that make one happy. If you have no relatives to get these things for you, usually you get in trouble trying to get them yourself.

White, 16, sexual delinquent.—When I see movies that show snappy clothes and wealth I do get dissatisfied. I want these things also. I want to have beautiful clothes, automobiles, and plenty of other luxuries that they have.

White, 16, sexual delinquent.—When I see movies like ——— ————, ———————, where you see snappy clothes, money, autos, etc., it makes me feel gaudy or dissatisfied and I crave for all these things. I want to leave the show right away, go out and make money, go to wild parties, dance every dance that comes around and have a good time.

White, 13, truant, runaway.—I saw a picture ——————— and ——————— had the most pretty evening gown on. It was a doll. It made me feel funny. I would like to be like her. The movies do make me want to have a great time like going horseback riding, airplane, and other games like the picture with ——————— in ———————.

White, 12, truant, runaway. — ————————————— made
me wish to be an actress, to wear pretty clothes, have swell
automobiles, yachts, go to swell places and be able to have
good times.

White, 15, truant, runaway.—The movies really do make me
long for nice clothes, nice home. And the way I really enjoy
being dressed is in a dress real long, about to your heels. Slip-
per pumps or a pair of slippers with a strap around the ankle;
a coat of velvet for the summer with a cape and a ruffle at the
bottom; for the winter a coat of some pretty cloth with real
nice fur on the collar and fur on the cuffs and a ruffle at the
bottom. This was taken from a picture I have seen and I still
remember the picture. But I don't remember its name.

White, 15, truant, runaway.—Not any picture so far has made
me disappointed with my home or family. But some have with
my clothes, for what I crave is expensive clothes and luxury;.
cars, all that goes with a queen life or what you may call the
"life of Riley." All my life I had a desire for beautiful and mag-
nificent clothes and I mostly envy ———————— and ——————————
in their clothes and the way they get those contrasting colors.

Seventy-one per cent of the sample of 252 delinquent
girls acknowledged that motion pictures make them want
to have fine clothes, automobiles, wealth, servants, etc.,
while 27 per cent indicate no such desire resulting from the
movies and 2 per cent did not respond to the question.

As has been intimated, the desire for luxury does not
necessarily lead to delinquency but that it may do so is
made quite clear by our materials. In the cases cited below of girls who ran away from home because of their desire for clothes, money, and a good time, it is significant
to note that in the first case the girl, separated from her
family, is easily led into a life of sexual delinquency. Running away from home on the part of young girls, of course, is
in itself an offense; consequently the second girl's escapade led
to her assignment to a truant and behavior-problem school.

White, 17, sexual delinquent.—I would love to have nice clothes and plenty of money and nothing to do but have a good time. When I see movies of that type, it makes me want to get out and go somewhere where things happen. Like the picture ———————————. The girls were nothing but adventuresses and look what great times they had. I always wanted to live with a girl chum. I saw many pictures where two or three girls roomed together. It showed all the fun they had. I decided I would, too. I ran away from home and lived with my girl friend but she was older than I and had different ideas and of course she led me and led me in the wrong way.

White, 15, truant, runaway.—The main reason I wanted to go away from home was because I thought I could make some money and get some clothes. I wanted nice things to make me look nice cause I always went out with girls whose parents had money and could give them anything that they needed. I've always longed to go to week-end parties like they have in the movies and go with fellows that have money and a good education and someone that would love me and be proud to have me for his wife. And to have maids and servants like they do in the movies and like the rich people do.

Twenty-seven per cent of the 252 girls stated that wanting fine clothes, automobiles, and wealth as shown in motion pictures led to their running away from home. This was denied by 67 per cent. Six per cent did not respond to the question. There is little doubt of a contributory influence of motion pictures in arousing desires for luxury and ambitions to enjoy them, in the case of the 27 per cent.

Especially powerful in leading to delinquent behavior is the combination of motion picture influence in creating a desire for a life of luxury and ease and suggesting manners for its achievement easily. To most of the delinquent girls and young women the achieving of patterns of luxury as depicted on the screen is impossible through ordinary conventional means. They are receptive, therefore, to easier methods of obtaining these often intensely desired luxuries.

Easier methods depicted on the screen that suggested themselves to many of the girls and young women often involve the exploitation of their sex.

White, 18, sexual delinquent.—Some of them (movies) make me dissatisfied with my own clothes. Most always I get what I want. Anyhow if it is in my power. Where there is a will there's a way. There are too many men in this world not to get what you want. There are plenty that are free and disengaged and want what you have got, which if they come after they can get. . . . They (movies) make me wish I had a car and lots of money and they also make me think how to make money. They tell me how to get it. There are several different ways of getting money; through sex, working, etc. Most always I get mine through sex.

White, 16, sexual delinquent.—In regard to ideas, there are two kinds of ideas, good and bad. The bad ideas I get from such pictures are to go out and have a high, rough-and-tumble life just like some of the rest. Go to a sporting house and make money and travel from one place to another.

Negro, 17, sexual delinquent.—When I ran away from here, I went to a show nearly every day, sometimes seeing the same show two or three times over. In this way I got to wanting to live the way the actresses lived. And so I used to go and get men to support me for a month or so and then change around and get me another man to live with.

White, 16, sexual delinquent.—When I see pictures with people who have snappy clothes, automobiles, etc., it makes me feel that I would like to have the clothes I see on the wearer. Movies of that sort make me feel that I would like to tear the clothes that I have on, right off. I often wish I had a good car like some of the actresses have. When I go out from here I am planning on getting a good car that I could go riding around in. I like to see movies where young girls and boys make a lot of money. I can think of over 100 ways of making money in your younger days, especially in the teens and twenties, with a slow or fast life. I think of making money, such as working in factories, doctor's office or any big office; but I can think of more ways in a fast life, which I will not mention because I've seen it done and have experienced it myself. Therefore I know something about it.

Of the group of 252 girls, 43 per cent stated that movies made them want to make a lot of money easily, 52 per cent indicated no such influence, while 5 per cent did not respond to the question. When asked to indicate the nature of the ideas suggested by the motion pictures for making money easily, 14 per cent of the 252 indicated "by gold-digging men"; 13 per cent by sexual delinquencies with men, and 25 per cent by living with a man and letting him support them. When asked if they ever did any of these things as a result of seeing movies to get easy money, 8 per cent of the girls indicated they followed out ideas of "gold digging"; 12 per cent admitted engaging in sexual delinquencies; and 18 per cent acknowledged they had lived with some man and let him support them.[6]

It seems clear that motion pictures may instill desires for luxury and a life of ease, which may lead to dissatisfaction with home, and indirectly to delinquency. Further, the desire for different forms of luxury may become so strong that some girls may adopt questionable methods as a means of realizing them.

D. IMITATION AND SEX DELINQUENCY

In the volume *Movies and Conduct* it is made clear that a high percentage of girls and young women imitate various forms of dress, make-up, and mannerisms portrayed

[6] That forms of delinquency other than sex exploitation are suggested by the movies and carried out by girls and young women is indicated by the following data. Seven per cent of the sample of 252 indicated that the movies gave them the idea of shoplifting as a means of easily securing money; and 9 per cent indicated the movies suggested gambling for this purpose. Four per cent of the girls admitted shoplifting and 8 per cent gambling to obtain money easily.

on the screen. The imitation of modes of beautification, mannerisms, and even techniques of love may in the main be a quite harmless and innocent form of activity. In our study of the imitation made by delinquent girls and young women, however, it becomes quite apparent that the copying of clothes, make-up, mannerisms, and particularly love techniques—flirting, kissing, hugging, etc.—may play an important part in their sexual delinquencies.

Let us begin by citing a few experiences chosen from the autobiographical accounts of the delinquent girls which show that motion pictures may be used as a source of information on clothes, mannerisms, and forms of conduct.

White, 15, truant, runaway.—The things I copied from the movies are clothes, talk, ways of dressing, ways of keeping my hair. The way of holding my hands when talking I copied from —————— from the picture ——————. I succeeded as far as I could see and I see that everybody liked my way of holding my hands. I tried to imitate —————— in holding her eyes when talking to someone, and I did succeed. But once I lost it when I intended to tell a lie and I did not succeed. I lowered my eyes instead of looking at the one I was talking to. Then once I tried to act like I was ——————. Kept my hair just like her, plucked my eyebrows in her way. Made up my face just like she makes up her face. I came to act like her when I saw the picture ——————. She looked so pretty and all her ways were so lovely that I believe everyone wanted to be like her. I succeeded as far as I could see, and I imitated her for the longest time. Until one day I changed and wanted to act like ——————. I kept my hair like hers, but I didn't succeed very far with her way.

White, 14, truant, runaway.—I have copied many things from the movies. I learned to make love, to smoke, and to wear swell clothes. I learned how to put on make-up and how to do different ways of make-up, and how to make my make-up and clothes go together. My girl friend is taking up dancing lessons, and I will as soon as I get out of here. There are many dances and steps I learned from —————————— and other stars—. . . . In the picture —————————— I learned to stay out late, to smoke and drink highballs, to do a few hot steps and make love.

White, 15, truant, runaway.—I have copied the way —————— —— acts and sits and smokes and dances. Well, I tried to do the same as her. . . . Well, ———————— likes swimming the best and so do I. I got the same kind of bathing suit that she has and shoes and hat and caps. I even dyed my hair red.

White, 16, sexual delinquent.—I like to see movies for I learn how to love, how to be neat, how to dress, manners of table, education, ways to attract men, etc.

White, 15, truant, runaway.—The way of flirting that I copied from ———————— was: When a fellow would smile at her she smiled back, and when the fellow would turn around she would stick up her nose at him. So I did the same and I got my girl friend to do it also. So we both kept it up or tried to imitate ———————— for about four months.

White, 18, sexual delinquent.—When you see the movies that throw hot and snappy parties it teaches you how to do it. And when you are invited out it shows you how things are nowadays.

White, 15, truant, runaway.—The movies taught me plenty of things; but I think I should be thankful for one thing and that is for the way of showing me how to act with a fellow and how to act with an older person, how to walk or ride with a fellow; when to apologize and when not to; when you are asked to dance with a fellow and another one has asked also, what to say to him then; or when you refuse to dance with one fellow and dance with another. They taught me that that was wrong— also if a fellow asked you to dance with him, and you didn't want to dance with him, have a good excuse.

In the report on *Movies and Conduct* some attention was given to the trial use, or testing out, of forms of behavior copied from motion pictures. This same feature of experimentation is noticeable in the accounts of imitation given by the delinquent girls. Since the significance of this experimentation is discussed in the above-mentioned report, we shall limit our treatment here to the citation of a single account to illustrate the point.

White, 15, truant, runaway.—When I saw ——————— in ——— ———————," I tried to fix my hair in the way she did. I kept at it for about a week and gave it up because my friends kept telling me I didn't look good that way. Another time I tried to copy ——————— in her love-making. I tried it on one of the boys I knew from school; just as I was getting him to the point where he would do anything I asked, he moved to Iowa and I had to start all over, but didn't succeed the second time. In the picture ———————, I tried to copy ——— ——— toughness and I went home and tried some rough stuff on my big brother and got knocked down for it; so I gave up the idea of even trying to be able to be like movie stars that were somewhat my ideal of women. When I went with a fellow to the show and saw ———————, this fellow put his arm around me and I felt so thrilled. So I let him kiss me. And in the middle of the pictures I put my arm around him. After the show we went home and sat on my front steps for a while and he asked me to meet him the next night and go to the show again that night. We saw ——————— and we went almost through all the scenes in the picture. I got a thrill out of that.

Of the group of 252 girls, 40 per cent stated that they imitated "how to act with a man" from the movies. Thirty per cent declared that they imitated ways of kissing, flirting, or making love from motion pictures.

The possibility of preparing oneself unwittingly for delinquency through the copying from motion pictures of forms of beautification, of love-making, and of forms of relations between young men and women, can perhaps be imagined from the accounts given so far. The imitation of "make-up" and dress may increase the attractiveness of the girl, or at least mark her as of the type that invites advances by young men. The use of forms of love-making, frequently passionate in character, may facilitate the breaking down of restraints.   Above all, the interpretation by many of the girls of what they see in motion pictures as forms of preliminary sex advances, may lead in their imitation of such patterns to questionable forms of conduct. In a scene, as many of the accounts show, the girls do not imitate merely separate, isolated items, but instead they tend to take over a framework of conduct marked by feelings of love, freedom, excitement, adventure, and wildness. In so far as such a general pattern serves as a source of information, or a guide to conduct, the copying may orient the girl in the direction of delinquency.

Some idea of this sort of effect can be seen in the following series of accounts.

White, Lithuanian parentage, 16, sexual delinquent.—Every girl is shy at her first meeting with boys. Because she does not know how to make love. Then is the time when you become more interested in passionate pictures because they teach you how to make love, dress, and how to act when you are with boys. Also to tell what kind of boys or girls you are with, whether the right or wrong kind. When it comes to making love and how to go about it. . . . I learned much and seemed to enjoy doing it. The older I grew the more I came in contact with boys and the more I tried to follow the movies. They gave me the first ideas of love, excitement, and adventure.

White, 17, sexual delinquent.—A good love picture makes things *more* interesting. I get the idea of how to make love, how to dress, and also what to do with myself when in a large crowd, especially young girls and boys. I am sure that there is no boy that wants a girl who doesn't know how to love, and there is no young girl that wants a boy that doesn't know how to love.

The first movie I attended with a fellow made me have a funny sensation down in my heart. It was the ————. I didn't know what to do with myself, that being the first movie I attended with a fellow. But oh! after seeing such a love picture

I wasn't shy and bashful from then on, because I sure did learn
how to make love from just seeing that one love picture. The
biggest *kick* that I get out of the movies that I see is learning
how to kiss, which makes me become very lovesick.

White, 17, sexual delinquent.—Movies taught me a lot per-
taining to men. They have taught me how to kiss, how a girl
should appear in the presence of her beau, how I should go
about loving with a fellow, how to lead up to sexual relations,
how to do hot dances, how to court, etc. A fellow is expected
to take his girl to movies, dances, skating parties, etc., and according to modern times he is expected to take her to a place,
whatever the circumstances may be, and have sexual relations
with her, and she is expected to show him a good time as he
shows her.

White, 16, sexual delinquent.—We go to the movies to get excited, thrilled, to learn something of how we should act in parties, etc. We go for amusement. We learn little bywords such
as "And how!" "Ain't you right!" "It's passable," etc. We
learn how to dress ourselves; we have to make a good appearance if we are going to have young men worth anything to make
love to us. Of course, this requires only cleanliness, decency,
you must be up to date. . . . I really don't think any boy would
want to go with a girl who didn't know how to make love, and
I don't know how a girl would want to go with a boy who didn't
know how to make love, do you? Movies teach us how to flirt.
. . . ——————— is a good play. It shows us some of
the latest styles; it gives you the idea of getting as much money
out of a man as you can, but it isn't as easy to practice in real
life as it seems. It shows you new steps in dancing, and new
songs. I like to see ——————— play because you can
always be sure and get the latest styles in clothes, new ways to
flirt, how to cheat men out of money, and etc.

White, Italian parentage, 18, sexual delinquent.—Then in the
opposite sex there was ——, the star of stars. I never missed
any of his pictures. In fact I saw many of them twice. He was
my ideal lover. Why can't the men take examples from him.
Believe me, if I was a man I would go to the movies and I would
learn how to make love. All the men think of is one thing, and

they head right for it. Now, if I was a man I would learn how
to make love, lead up to the point slow but sure; and when they
did get it, believe me, they would love it. After we'd seen ———
I used to go with a boy that thought the same as I did of ———
We would go for a stroll; and I'd just wish I had someone to
love me as ——— does, and he wished he could learn the great
art of loving as well as ——— pictured it. In this way we'd share
the greatest of love. What the men call a love, I'd call a rape
case, coarse and common—nothing lovable about it. The trouble
with them is they just think about themselves; as long as they're
satisfied, they don't give a darn.

To summarize and make more clear the material in this
section it is important to note that the imitation of modes
of beautification and mannerisms to appear more attractive to men, the imitation of unconventional motion-picture definitions of relations of the sexes and conduct in
the presence of members of the opposite sex, and the imitation of love technique, may individually and collectively,
especially when accompanied by sexual possession, dispose
or lead to sexual misconduct.

E. Imitation and Non-Sexual Delinquency

Of the delinquent girls from whom material was secured
in the course of this study, few were charged with forms
of delinquency other than those of sex misconduct and
truancy. Our materials, however, have yielded a few instances where motion pictures have displayed forms of
crime or of questionable conduct which were copied, and have
led to delinquency other than that of sex or truancy. We
are giving a few of the accounts.

White, 16, sexual delinquent.—When I first started to run
around I was only 11. At this time I was living in ———, Illinois
My girl friend, G——, and I usually went to the theaters by
ourselves. We would sneak out and go to shows whenever we
could scrape up enough money, and we usually got it some place

After the movies were over we'd go out and try to imitate the actors. Usually we'd go out and find us a guy. In the movies we'd see girls shoplifting and doing many other clever things. We would then go out and try these things. While we were living in ———— these things went along very successfully.

White, 17, high-school junior.—Once when I was little, though, I did get some terrible temptations from the movies. I had seen during that year several movies of the criminal type. Pictures of men breaking into banks and pictures of shoplifters began to interest me. I studied them intensely, never dreaming the rut I was getting into. Before I fully realized what I was doing I found that I had taken several minor things such as balls, etc., from the ten-cent store. It began on a small scale either with shoplifting or with taking pennies or small change that was lying around. Then one day as I grew more experienced in the technique I increased the amount to a dollar bill. Well, I don't have to enlarge on the next event, because I guess that you probably have gotten severe punishment for one cause or another. It isn't necessary to say that I never stole another thing.

Negro, 17, sexual delinquent.—The movies weren't very important in getting me here, but when I saw ———————— in ———————————, I began gambling and everything.

White, 15, truant, runaway.—I liked plays about gangland and rum runners; well, during the time my sister was at S—— I saw a play called ————————————. I can't recall the cast but anyway it was about speakeasies and other places, but mostly I was mostly interested in speakeasies. There were waitresses in the play. Now I recall the name of one of the waitresses—it was ————————. I thought to myself it would be fun to be a waitress in one of these places. So one day I was telling M—— M——, that was our neighbor, about it; he said to me, "Don't you people know that I run a beer flat?" I said, "Why no." So he promised me a job, if I promised not to tell the neighbors, but tell them that I am doing the housework for his wife. So I did, but it was such a surprise to me I wanted to tell the world. I thought it was such a great thing, but it was fun to know you were breaking the laws. It was just my luck, though, two weeks after I quit his place was raided. That's one good consolation anyway. It gave me a desire to be a runner of a beer flat.

Although these non-sexual forms of delinquency occur relatively infrequently in the cases studied, the fact that 8 per cent of 252 inmates acknowledged that they have imitated shoplifting shown in the movies and 9 per cent gambling indicates that motion picture influences in this connection are by no means insignificant.[7]

F. Competing Attraction of Motion Pictures

Our treatment of the major ways in which motion-picture experiences seem to have influenced the delinquent careers of girls has been confined to the content of what is displayed. There is another relation which appears significantly in our materials—the way in which motion pictures, because of their attraction, may compete with home and school. It is fitting that some attention be devoted to this relation before concluding this chapter.

We have pointed to the cases of a number of girl delinquents who have been led to truancy and running away from home because of the desire to enjoy a life of gayety, romance, and adventure and achieve the luxury, clothes, leisure, etc., shown in motion pictures. In a number of instances, the mere desire to attend motion pictures led to conflicts with parents, to truancy, and occasionally to running away from home. Some girls prefer attending motion pictures to going to school; and sometimes, frequent attendance leads to difficulties with parents that culminate in running away. Such behavior points to the fascination which motion pictures have for certain young girls, and shows how motion pictures may conflict with the interests of other institutions.

[7] The "girl bandit," a comparatively modern phenomenon, has not been studied in this investigation.

In the interests of space, the illustration of this point will be confined to two cases.

White, 15, truant, runaway.—One reason I went away from school was I enjoyed movies better than school. I got my money from my parents for lunch. So instead of going to school, I made some excuse and went to the movies instead. And while I was not in school I would pick up a lift and go out for a little ride until the shows opened. Then after the show I walked a little ways; then picked up a lift and went home about 3:30, just as if I had just come from school. My mother never knew it. One of the times as I was coming out of the show I met a boy friend I knew. So I took in another one with him and came out about 8:30. This was too late to go home from school. So instead of taking me home I had him take me to a girl friend's. That evening I didn't go home. The next evening I and my girl friend went out. This was the second night I was away from home. I kept on going out day after day and didn't go home for a whole month.

White, 14, truant, runaway.—When I was 10 years old I fell so much in love with the movies that I begged and begged my mother to give me money for the show, but she wouldn't. She said it would ruin my life, if I went to the movies so often. But as she didn't give me any money, I would be a sneak and take the money off the table and go to the movie. When I came home at nine or ten o'clock in the evening my ma was waiting for me with a big strap. Every time my mother wouldn't give me any money for the movies I'd go to the shelf where she kept her money or I would go to her purse and take 50 cents and go to the movie from one in the afternoon till 11:00 or 11:30 in the evening, which spoiled me very much. Of course my parents had to do something as I didn't obey them as I was supposed to. I very often quarreled with my mother. She told me that movies weren't good for me. I told her they were. She said they were filthy and sloppy for girls like me. Of course, I didn't mind her. I kept doing what I wanted to. I didn't want anybody to be boss over me. I ran away from home just because of a quarrel with my mother about the movies. When I did leave home, day and night my place was in the movies and I never stopped going until I was put in an institution where they didn't let the girls go to a show. But I didn't stay long enough to know the place well, for I ran away from there. When I did run away I stayed out. . . . That's what stopped me from going to school. *The movies.* They spoiled me very much. Of course, when they took me to the Juvenile Court, the judge as usual asked my truant officer what kept me from school. My mother opened up, "Why the movies, of course."

Some understanding of the extent to which motion pictures may compete with other institutions for the attention of young girls is given in the statistical data secured in response to the questionnaire given to the 252 delinquent girls. Fifty-four per cent of this number stated that they had stayed away from school to go to the movies. Forty-four per cent indicate this not to have been true in their cases, while 2 per cent did not respond to the question. Thirty-five per cent declare they had quarrels with parents over motion-picture attendance. Sixty-four per cent stated this was not true in their case, while 1 per cent did not reply to the question. Furthermore, 17 per cent of the girls acknowledge they had run away from home after quarreling with their parents over motion-picture attendance; 79 per cent declare this was not true in their cases, while 4 per cent did not respond to the question.

Over half of the delinquents studied, then, it appears at some time have been truant from school to attend movies; over one third of them have had conflict with their parents over motion-picture attendance and almost one fifth of them have run away from home after such difficulties.

It will be well to remember, again, as we have stated above, that truancy and running away from home may be the introduction to a series of experiences which result in more serious forms of delinquency. In so far as motion pictures by their attraction draw away the allegiance of girls from the stable institutions which surround them, they may help to prepare the way for delinquency.

G. SUMMARY

It is evident that the motion pictures play an important rôle in the lives of delinquent girls and young women. A restatement of the questionnaire responses will help to make this clear. Twenty-five per cent of the sample of 252 delinquent girls studied, mainly from 14 to 18 years of age, stated they had engaged in sexual relations with men following the arousing of sex impulses by a passionate love picture. Forty-one per cent admit that going to wild parties, cabarets, roadhouses, etc., "like they do in the movies," "got them into trouble." More specifically, 38 per cent of them say that they were led, in their attempts to live a wild, gay, fast life such as presented in the movies, to stay away from school; 33 per cent were led to run away from home; 23 per cent were led to sexual delinquencies. In their efforts to enjoy clothes, automobiles, lives of luxury and ease as depicted on the screen, 27 per cent have been led on occasion to run away from home. In their efforts to achieve a life of luxury easily through means suggested, at least in part, by motion pictures, 18 per cent say that they have lived with a man and let him support them; 12 per cent that they have engaged in other forms of sexual delinquency; 8 per cent that they have been led to "gold-dig" men; 8 per cent have been led to gamble; and 4 per cent that they have engaged in shoplifting. Fifty-four per cent of the girls declared they have stayed away from school to go to movies; and 17 per cent that they have run away from home after conflict with their parents over frequent motion picture attendance.

To this series of declarations, which represent an acknowledgment of the influence of motion pictures on delinquency, may be added another set of statistical data which cover experiences which, while they do not represent forms of delinquency, might easily help to dispose girls in that direction. Forty-eight per cent of the 252 girls studied admit feeling like having a man make love to them after they have seen a passionate love picture. Thirty-nine per cent stated that they invited men to make love to them and "pet" them after witnessing such pictures. Seventy-two per cent stated that they improved their attractiveness to men by imitation of clothes, hair-dress, make-up, etc.; and 30 per cent that they imitated techniques of flirting, kissing, or making love. Forty-nine per cent acknowledged that movies made them want to live a gay, fast life; 41 per cent admit that movies have instilled desires to go to wild parties, cabarets, and roadhouses. Seventy-one per cent reveal that motion pictures have made them want fine clothes, automobiles, wealth, servants, etc.; and 43 per cent indicate pictures have made them want to make a lot of money easily. Thirty-nine per cent stated that they daydreamed of lives of luxury and ease; 26 per cent of gay, fast life, wild parties, cabarets, etc.; 32 per cent of having a man make love to them as they do in the motion pictures; and 7 per cent of being a vampire or "gold-digger." Finally, 35 per cent indicated that they had conflicts with their parents over motion picture attendance.

It seems clear from the statistical data and from the autobiographical accounts that motion pictures are of importance, both directly and indirectly, in contributing to female delinquency.

CHAPTER VI

THE DETERRENT AND REFORMATIVE IN-
FLUENCE OF MOTION PICTURES

ONE of the most interesting problems of the relation of motion pictures to crime is that of deterrency. In most pictures which deal with crime, the criminal suffers ultimately some punishment or comes to some untimely end. In fact, it has been asserted frequently by representatives of the producers of motion pictures that crime pictures are consciously planned to show the eventual retribution which comes to the criminal as a result of his wrongdoing. Their claim has been that motion pictures discourage crime by stressing the eventual ill-fate suffered by the criminal. In view of what is ostensibly a conscious effort, it is interesting to study the extent of their success in accomplishing this purpose. This, of course, is just part of a larger setting, for there are other pictures besides those which treat crime which presumably may check criminal or delinquent tendencies.

Our materials show that motion pictures may play some part in the prevention of delinquency or crime chiefly in these ways: by playing on the sentiments of individuals, thereby arousing impulses "to be good"; by depicting criminal or delinquent careers as unattractive and dangerous; and by vivid portrayal of punishment of the offenders. Let us take up these three forms in the order in which we have mentioned them.

A. The Impulse to Be Good

In the report, *Movies and Conduct*, some attention was paid to the way in which certain kinds of motion pictures may appeal to the sentiments of individuals and arouse within them impulses and intentions of being "good." Usually pictures which induce sorrow, such as those showing the distress occasioned a mother by the behavior of a wayward son, or those which play upon religious sentiments, lead to this effect. Some idea of the extent of this experience is presented by the following statistical information.

Seventy per cent of a sample of 440 grade-school boys think that the movies make boys and girls "do good things." Sixty-nine per cent of a sample of 435 grade-school girls think likewise, and a somewhat smaller percentage of a sample of 139 boys—53 per cent—in a truant and behavior school think motion pictures make boys and girls do good things. When asked what types of pictures make them want to be good, 27 per cent of the truant and behavior-problem boys, 29 per cent of the grade-school boys in the high-rate delinquency areas, 24 per cent of the boys in the medium-rate delinquency areas, and 13 per cent of the boys in the low-rate delinquency areas indicated religious or moral pictures had this effect. Four per cent of the truant and behavior-problem boys, 9 per cent of the high-rate delinquency area boys, 7 per cent of the medium-rate delinquency area boys, and 4 per cent of the low-rate delinquency area boys indicated that gangster or crime pictures made them want to be good.

In the case of the grade-school girls, 38 per cent of the girls living in the high-rate delinquency area, 24 per cent in the medium-rate delinquency areas, and 14 per cent in the low-rate delinquency areas indicated that religious or moral pictures made them want to be good, while only 1 per cent of the girls in the high-rate delinquency area, 4 per cent in the medium-rate delinquency areas, and none of the girls in the low-rate delinquency areas indicated that gangster or crime pictures had this effect.

Similarly, 79 per cent of the sample of 252 inmates of a state training school for delinquent girls indicated that movies have made them want to be "real good"; while 18 per cent do not acknowledge such an influence; and 3 per cent did not answer the question.   When asked to indicate what type of picture made them want to be good, 45 per cent said moral, religious, or sentimental pictures had this effect, while 25 per cent were influenced in this manner by crime or gangster pictures or pictures which show the ill fate of women who go wrong.

It is significant to note the contrast between the effects of religious, moral, or sentimental pictures and crime pictures showing the punishment or ill fate of offenders in inclining school boys and girls and the delinquent girls to be good.   The punishment and ill fate of offenders apparently does not have the appeal of moral, sentimental, or religious pictures in inviting the desire "to be good."

Usually the "desire to be good" which is aroused by motion pictures is short-lived.   Of the 54 truant and behavior-problem boys who responded to the question, 35 per cent indicated that the movies made them stay good for less than one day, 28 per cent for one day to a week, 20 per cent from one week to a month, 13 per cent from one month to a year, and 4 per cent for over a year.   Thus, 83 per cent of the truant and behavior-problem boys indicated that although some pictures they had seen made them want to be "real good," they remained good as a result of the picture for a period of less than one month.   Of the 191 boys of the three areas combined who answered the question, 14 per cent indicated that the movies made them stay good for less than one day, 26 per cent from one day to a week, 28 per cent from one week to a month, 16 per cent from one month to a year, and 16 per cent for over a year. In other words, 68 per cent indicated the movies made them stay good for a period of less than one month.

Of the 148 girls of the three areas combined who answered the question, 10 per cent indicated the movies made them stay good for less than one day, 21 per cent from one day to a week, 24 per cent from one week to a month, 22 per cent from one month to a year, and 24 per cent for over a year. Fifty-five per cent of the girls, although they indicated some pictures made them want to be "real good," said they remained good for a period of less than one month.

Of the 191 delinquent girls who answered this question, 16 per cent acknowledge that motion pictures made them stay good for about a day; 19 per cent for about a week; 19 per cent for about a month; 22 per cent for about a year; and 24 per cent for more than a year. Thus, about 54 per cent admitted staying good for a period of about one month or less.

Fifty-one per cent of a sample of 110 male inmates acknowledged they have seen movies which made them want to be real good and to "go straight"; 36 per cent indicated no such influence, while 13 per cent did not respond to the question.

Basing our remarks merely on these questionnaire responses, it seems that although some pictures make boys and girls, delinquents and non-delinquents, want to be "real good," the immediate traceable effect is on the whole temporary, of longer duration among girls than boys and among non-delinquent boys than delinquent boys.

B. CRIMINAL CAREERS AS UNATTRACTIVE AND DANGEROUS

By depicting the unattractive and dangerous aspects of the lives of delinquents and criminals motion pictures may exercise some deterrent influence.   The portrayal of the dangerous life and perhaps death of gangsters seems to be especially effective in discouraging boys and young men from such careers.   The depiction of the hardships of wayward women—disease, illegitimacy, deformed offspring, social ostracism, etc.—serves the same purpose among girls and young women.   Pictures of this type tend to teach a lesson and put the individual on guard.

Male, white, 23, sentenced for burglary, inmate of reformatory.— I have never had the idea of being a gangster because of the pictures I have seen where they take a gangster for a ride.   That put a scare in me because I value my life.

Male, white, Italian, 13, high-rate delinquency area.—"I used to like best to see de gangster get caught robbin something. I saw de 'Big House' and 'Paid.'   De 'Big House' was good because it told about two pals and in de end dey kill each other. I wanted to see it twice or three times.   I didn't feel like I'd like to be a big shot cause I'm fraid of getting killed."

Male, white, Italian, 16, high-rate delinquency area.—"I kinda like gangster movies now.   I like de actors dat play in em like Wallace Beery, but I don't get no good out of dem.   They make me feel dat crime don't pay.   I never feel like I'd like to be like dem—de're king for a few days and den down dey go wit de rest of dem."

Male, white, sentenced for burglary, inmate of state training school.—I saw a play in which a gangster got double-crossed and killed.   A plain-clothes cop was always telling him to get away and not go with that gang.   Well, this guy didn't listen to him so he got bumped off.   After I saw that play I began to think it over and I said I better take it easy or else I will get bumped off.

Female, white, 16, sexual delinquent.—Movies were not to blame by any means for my misbehavior. It was when I'd see passionate plays, I'd go home and then resolve to behave. The girls always became diseased and then if they had a child it was blind or deformed. These plays always seemed to teach me a lesson. . . . When I see pictures of women going wrong I think that I'll behave because I wouldn't want a terrible disease and if I had a child I wouldn't want it to be blind or deformed. I certainly do think that such pictures are true to life.

Female, white, 16, sexual delinquent.—I get ideas of how a criminal leads his life from a murder or mystery picture. They go through many a dangerous scene of being shot or caught. Some have love affairs and bring the girl into it somehow, either to watch or break in houses, and by having love affairs with some such fool. Of course, after the fellows get what they are after, they desert the girl so that she can make a living the best she knows how. We learn how we come to help criminals. Then what becomes of us? While we are offered the love and jewels (which is a girl's one desire) we do not realize what we will go through or how it will turn out. It gives us a warning that if we are offered jewels to refuse. . . I take notice of the warning which is in the picture.

Female, white, 14, truant, runaway.—A play I saw, namely, "Is Your Daughter Safe?", for adults, has taught me how to beware of boys, especially if I should ever take a pick-up ride, which I have taken only once. Well, this play taught me— and now I know the jokes that fellows play on some girls. They take girls out sometimes and make them walk—that's if they're good girls, they'll walk.

Forty-four per cent of a sample of 110 male inmates of a large state reformatory acknowledge that they feel convinced that the risks and dangers of being a gangster are too great when they see an adventuresome burglar or bandit picture. Fifty per cent of the sample of 252 delinquent girls indicate the movies taught them the woman always pays the price for a good time; 47 per cent acknowledge that motion pictures taught them not to be sexually delinquent because they might have a child or get diseased; 49 per cent that wild life does not pay. In this connection 55 per cent indicated movies taught them to beware of boys and men because all they want from a girl is sex.

Although the hold of these lessons may be brief (45 per cent of the delinquent girls declared they forgot about them when they were with men), the questionnaire material suggests that motion pictures may deter young men and young women from delinquency and crime by depicting the unattractiveness and danger of these forms of life.

C. Fear of Ill Fate of Offenders and Punishment

Instilling fear of punishment seems to be the most effective way in which motion pictures may deter individuals from delinquency and crime. The portrayal of long periods of incarceration and of the monotonous routine life of penal institutions and of punishment by death sentences makes its imprint on the minds of both delinquent and non-delinquent observers. In many instances it is evident that criminals or delinquents may be hesitant about, or even deterred from, the commission of some crimes as a result of memories of what was seen in motion pictures.

Male, white, 24, sentenced for burglary, inmate of reformatory.— A picture I consider very interesting and inspiring to the criminal in the line of his profession is "London After Midnight." This picture has a cast of daring gangsters and murderers. I took a great liking to this picture as it was very exciting. This picture kept the law on the go as there were daring crimes committed throughout. Like every other crook picture, the criminal is caught and punished. This picture taught me that a fellow can't fool with the law too long. . . . I'll always bear in mind that a tough guy will exist until the law puts the "dampers" on him, although he may lead the life of a prince. The movies always have the crooks brought to justice at the end of their underworld pictures. I am for more of this sort. The above explains what I have gotten out of movies and so I think I will include this information also. An exciting picture gives me many thrills throughout its showing. I hardly think it causes me to do daring things, although I bear in mind the ways they show of getting easy money, committing murder, etc., and finally of how the law takes a hand in the crime. Several times before I would start to commit a crime, I would often think of the penalty I would have to pay if I were caught. This thought has come to me again and again, and I'm sure it has saved me from committing many crimes. "The Drag Net," "Ladies of the Mob," and "You Can't Win" are great pictures for a fellow to learn vital lessons from.

Male, white, 22, sentenced for robbery, inmate of reformatory.— There are many pictures which are pretty sentimental and show it doesn't pay to try and be a tough gangster in this world because you're always bound to get caught sooner or later. A greater majority of the gangster pictures show that it doesn't pay to commit a crime because a person's bound to pay in the end. . . . I can't explain what the pictures were about but some inner feeling in me made me think things over when I see them kind of pictures and go straight. The picture showed the life of a criminal and all his hardships and losses and it also showed a part of where he actually was doing time in a prison. The prison and its steady daily routine and discipline is enough to make a person hesitate before he commits a crime.

Male, white, 15, sentenced for robbery, inmate of state training school.—Once I saw a picture where some brave guys went out and struck up a bank and got away with thousands of dollars and the car they were in went dead and they just sat in the car instead of getting out and running and the cops got them and sent them to jail. When they had their trial the judge sentenced them to the pen. I have forgotten the name of the picture now because it happened quite a while ago.

Sometimes I would see a picture and if it would be like that one that I just told you about, it would make me feel that I had better go straight or I would land up in the penitentiary. I would hesitate about pulling a job because I would be a little leary of the law. When I see a picture or a burglar in a picture and he gets his time I don't feel so good because I might get the same if I would commit the crime, but other times I hardly care anything about it.

Female, white, 16, sexual delinquent.—The punishment that I see they receive does make me want to go out and lead a good life. Because I feel that nine women out of ten who go wrong *always* pay in the end.

Female, white, 16, sexual delinquent.—I wouldn't like to be like these women that go wrong. The punishment and bad endings of such plays do make me feel as if I want to stay out of trouble.

Sixty-nine per cent of the boys in a school for truants and behavior-problems, 69 per cent of the grade-school boys in high-rate delinquency areas, 71 per cent in medium-rate delinquency areas, and 77 per cent in low-rate delinquency areas think that punishment of "bad men" meted out in the movies stops boys and girls from doing "bad things." Seventy per cent of the girls in the high-rate delinquency areas, 64 per cent in the medium-rate delinquency areas, and 68 per cent in the low-rate delinquency areas feel the same to be true.

Forty-nine per cent of the male convict sample of 110 think that punishment given to the criminal in the movies is likely to stop one from committing crime. Forty-three per cent think it is not, while 8 per cent did not express an opinion. Twenty-six per cent of the same inmate sample indicated that punishment as shown in the movies had made them at one time or another hesitate about committing a crime. Fifty-six per cent indicated that this was not true in their case, while 18 per cent did not answer the question.

Of the 252 delinquent girls and young women studied, 51 per cent indicate that the ill fate of women who go wrong in the movies has kept them from doing things people think are not right. Although the number of male and female inmates who say that motion pictures are likely to deter individuals from delinquent acts is greater than those who admit being deterred themselves, we find that 26 per cent of the male and 51 per cent of the female delinquents state that they were deterred at one time or another by the punishment or fate of criminals as shown in motion pictures.[1]

D. NULLIFYING AND IMMUNIZATION INFLUENCES

There are a number of situations and nullifying factors which may counteract the deterrent influence of motion pictures. In some cases the deterrent influence is short-lived; the feeling to be good, the unattractive insight into criminal life, or the fear of punishment wearing off rapidly and being completely forgotten. In other cases the deterrent effect of motion pictures disappears in tempting situations or under the pressure of an individual's gang or associates. Many observers get accustomed to the portrayal of the dangers and unattractive aspects of the criminal career and to the inevitable punishment of movie offenders. Others feel that punishment in the movies is not made vivid enough, the hardships and sufferings of the criminal never being actually presented. Some discount the pictures, feeling they are not true to life, and fail to be affected in any way by them. Many feel that, although the offender is shown as apprehended and punished, they themselves can outwit the law and succeed in their criminal enterprises. In some instances, the sympathy of observers is aroused

---

[1] We have no instance in our materials where an individual was completely deterred from a delinquent or criminal career through the influence of motion pictures. This should not be taken to mean that no such cases exist.

by the portrayal of the consequences of criminal behavior, leading them to feel sorry for the offender and missing what is meant to be a deterrent influence. Finally, some are emotionally aroused by the showing of the punishment and ill fate of delinquents and criminals and bitterly resent such pictures. Under these circumstances the deterrent influence of motion pictures becomes nil.

Let us now present findings which make these points clear. For purposes of convenience to the reader they will be presented under their appropriate headings in terms of the factors and situations discussed above.

1. *Short life of deterrent effect.*—The intention to be good may be instilled by motion pictures, but it may also be almost immediately forgotten. In the first case cited the individual committed the crime for which he was incarcerated shortly after resolving "to be good and to go straight."

Male, white, 23, sentenced for burglary, inmate of state reformatory.—I have not had any experience in which the movies have made me hesitate in pulling a job, for this is my first time in trouble, but I have seen in the movies where the fellows pulled the job and they most always got caught and put in prison, and that is the last place that I ever wanted to be, and that was what made me want to be good and go straight.

Male, white, 34, sentenced for robbery, ex-convict.—Movies, I don't think, could make one go straight. Sad pictures sometimes make me think a good deal, but after you get back out on the street, you have other things to think about. This world goes too fast and one doesn't get enough time to think. He acts, does things, and thinks afterwards. Everything is done on the spur of the moment. A couple of nights ago I was on my way home fully intentioned to go to bed; on the way I passed a joint, went in, and got drunk. There you are, proof of what I say. People don't think about anything; they do it and answer questions afterwards. Check yourself and you'll find what I say is true.

Male, white, 16, charged with robbery.[2]—

Q. Did you see any of Al Jolson's pictures?

A. Yes sir. I saw him in "Sonny Boy" and "Say It With Songs."

Q. Did they make you cry?

A. I know one of them did. I don't know which one it was.

Q. When you see a picture like that, does it make you want to be good?

A. I have the intention of being good, but after I get out of the show, I forget all about it. I've gone to bed plenty of nights thinking over it. Next morning I forget all about it.

Male, white, 17, charged with burglary.[2]—

Q. Do you ever remember hesitating to go out on a job because of some picture that you saw?

A. Yes. The last couple of nights I never wanted to go out. Then the other kids started off and drew me right after them.

Q. Do you remember any of the pictures that made you hesitate?

A. Well, there was Al Jolson in "The Singing Fool."

Q. Did that make you want to be better?

A. Yes.

Q. Did you cry when you saw that picture?

A. No, I never cry for any picture.

Q. You did feel like being good?

A. Sure.

Q. How long did you feel that way?

A. Till the next Sunday.

Q. When did you see the picture?

A. That was about on a Tuesday.

2. *Yielding to temptation or pressure.*—The possibility of punishment or suffering as portrayed in the movies and deterrent influences set in motion may be completely submerged in the mind of the individual in a tempting situation, or they may be overcome by group pressure in the gang situation.

[2] These two boys, members of the same gang, were interviewed separately. It is interesting to note their corroborative responses in their reaction to the same picture.

Female, white, 16, sexual delinquent.—When I see pictures of "women that go wrong" I often think of myself before I came to this place. I thought that I was just it and could do everything I saw others do. Some lives that I see some women lead do not suit me. I don't think that I would want to lead that sort of life they do. Some of the punishment that comes to some of these women never affected me or helped to keep me from trouble. Because when I got out with a fellow I forgot all about the movies I had seen.

Male, white, 20, sentenced for burglary, inmate of state reformatory.—Whenever I would see a play where the crook was caught, red-handed, or when the cops would trail the crook till he had to give himself up or keep in hiding, it made me hesitate in doing a job. Also, it would make me think twice before I pulled a job, when I saw the crook getting the third degree (beating and knocking about). It also influenced me to go straight, but every time I saw easy money in sight, I couldn't resist the temptation of trying to get it.

Male, white, 23, sentenced for robbery, inmate of state reformatory.—Several times while we were in the pursuit of such adventures I would stop and think about the boy's mother that I had seen in some picture who was very poor and was leading a hand-to-mouth existence. Then I would wonder whether the boy whom we had selected as a victim (to be robbed) had a mother who was also in such dire circumstances. My heart would be stirred with deep compassion for the unfortunate lad, and I would remonstrate with my companions to release him, but they would only laugh at me and admonish me not to be so "chicken-hearted," that it was all in the game. By that time I would have a change of heart and would enter into the undertakings with all my former fervor and zest. I would content myself with the thought that perhaps the boy's mother was not as impoverished as I at first feared.

3. *Getting accustomed to the punishment shown.*—In some cases delinquents, at first deterred by the portrayal of punishment in the movies, become accustomed to it and no longer are affected by it. It is interesting to note that

one who becomes indifferent to the deterrent influences of the picture may get from it "new ideas of how to pull a job or fool the police" or see only "the jolly-go-lucky times."

Female, white, 16, sexual delinquent.—What about women who go wrong? Hmm. I'm so damn used to that that it's all immaterial to me as to what happens. It's too bad a kid can't go out once in a while and have a good time without having to pay for it. . . . The kind of life such a woman leads in the movies makes me want to be like them. To join the gangsters and have a jolly-go-lucky time. Working in a roadhouse and having a wild time with a wild, care-free gang of buddies.

No!!! the bad endings these women get don't make me feel like keeping out of trouble after I get out. These movies up here don't make an impression on me like that. Because these movies we see here are not like the ones I crave. These up here do not have the stuff in them like the ones on the outside. Oh, gosh! only for another chance on the outside I would show these people up here what effect a good movie has on me.

Female, white, 18, sexual delinquent.—When I see pictures about women who "go wrong" it only makes me wish I was in their place. It seems as that is what I like to do. It makes me worse because I do know what thrill and pleasures they get about going wrong. Some say different, but I have a better feeling when I do wrong things than when I do right, especially in passionate ways. . . . I go right ahead and take my punishment like a sport. . . . Some say you don't feel right when you are in trouble. I don't feel right when I am not in.

Male, white, 20, sentenced for robbery, inmate of reformatory.— Whenever I saw a show about the bad guy being caught it made me scared and hesitate at first but I soon got used to it and never minded it any more. I don't think I could name any of the pictures but I sure enjoyed them just the same. One good play I saw was the "Big House." My feeling towards a burglar or gangster is that I always wish that they'd make a safe get-away. Many of these pictures are true to life and many of them are just plays. I feel "rotten" whenever I see the burglar get sent "up the river" or get shot. I always like to see him make his get-away. I also hold a grudge against the cops that sent him up. Many of the cops give him a bum rap just to get him out of the way. . . . I felt sorry for a fellow who gets captured in a crime picture. Most of them give me new ideas of how to pull jobs and fool the police. Pictures like this don't stop me from pulling another job. I always think I can get away with it and so I keep right at it.

4. *Punishment not made vivid.*—In some cases delinquents claim they are not deterred by motion pictures because the punishment of the criminal is not portrayed vividly and makes no impression on them. Not only are the sufferings of the offender—the worry, fear, long sentences, monotony and hardships of prison life, etc.—not realistically depicted, but in some instances the prison life shown is not without attraction or appeal.

Male, white, 17, charged with burglary.—
Q. What do you think is the effect of the punishment which the criminal usually gets in the movies?
A. Well, when they catch him, I see sometimes it shows one day and the next day, and then about six years go by, but I never think about their sentence. I don't think it's bad.
Q. The punishment he gets doesn't make any impression?
A. No. Because they don't really show what he has to suffer. It shows they play baseball, and what they get to eat and things like that.
Q. It never shows them in their cells?
A. Only once in a while.

Male, white, 19, sentenced for robbery, inmate of state reformatory.—In the majority of the pictures the gangster gets killed in the last reel after battling with the upholders of the law, but in the other cases where he is not killed he is caught and handcuffed and sent on his way to the penitentiary. I don't remember ever seeing a picture where the gangster was sentenced and I don't know how much time he received, so I am unable to state whether his term of incarceration was sufficient, not enough, or too much.

5. *Discounting of the pictures.*—Delinquents and criminals may develop a sophistication and emotional detachment [3] to punishment óf offenders in motion pictures. This may be due to a feeling that after all movies are meant primarily for entertainment, or to the feeling that motion pictures are not true to life. The latter notion frequently arises when the personal experience of the individual contradicts the movie theme that "crime does not pay."

Male, white, 22, sentenced for robbery, inmate of reformatory.— No picture has ever made me hesitate about doing anything, and nothing outside of a girl has ever made me want to be good, go straight for any length of time. When I see a gangster picture, I see two sides of it. I see the part that is true to life, and I also see the other. Such things as bribing a cop, taking a guy for a ride or bumping him off on the street and the copper's pigeon or rat is true to life and the rest I pass up as immaterial. In movies usually the crook gets killed or gets enough time to keep him in the rest of his life, but that is not true to life.

Male, white, 20, sentenced for burglary, inmate of state reformatory.—When I see a gangster or burglar picture, I think some of it is true and some of it is not. When they catch the criminal the criminal doesn't get as much punishment as it seems. I do one job and don't get caught and I think I can do another job.

Male, white, 27, sentenced for robbery, ex-convict.—I enjoy all pictures but criminal and crime flashes. They do not appeal to me. I hate to see anyone punished. The moral of all criminal pictures is the wrongdoer gets caught, which is only true in about 9% of true life crime.

Male, white, 24, sentenced for burglary, inmate of state reformatory.—Whenever I see a gangster picture my sympathy is always with the gangster (unless he happens to be one of the odious kind) and I am always wishing that he will have success in his undertakings and make a clean get-away. But that very seldom happens in pictures and usually when it does happen the gangster gets caught (or killed) in the last reel and made to pay the

[3] See *Movies and Conduct.*

penalty for his atrocious crimes. While I am watching the picture I am oblivious to my surroundings, and imagine myself to be in the gangster's place who is participating in the picture. Of course, after it is all over I come to earth again and realize it's only fun and made simply for entertainment.

6. *Feeling they can outwit the law.*—A feeling common to many delinquents and criminals is the conviction that although offenders in movies are usually apprehended and punished *they* can outwit the law. They often assert the movie criminals are caught only because they make mistakes which they themselves can avoid. Many criminals hope to "pull a few good jobs," get away with it, and then "quit the racket."

Male, white, 20, sentenced for burglary, inmate of reformatory.—Sometimes I would like to see robbers make a big job and get away with it, but in time they would get caught. In the picture I would see ways of getting away from the cops. I would like to be the robber and make the big haul and get away and not be so foolish as to let the cops get me as they did.

Male, white, Italian, 15, high-rate delinquency area.—"I feel dat when dey are going to the electric chair when dey get caught and I feel dat dey shouldn't have done it den, but waited till de coast was clear."

Male, white, 14, charged with burglary, awaiting trial.—
Q. What do you think is the effect on boys of the punishment which the criminal gets in the pictures?
A. In lots of underworld pictures, they don't get caught at all. Sometimes they do.
Q. Do you happen to remember any of those pictures?
A. No.
Q. How about those pictures where they do get caught? Do you think that tends to stop you from stealing?
A. Every time we see one we don't care. We thought we wouldn't get caught. We were going to make a good place and then quit.

7. *Feeling of sympathy for criminals.*[4]—The portrayal of the criminal fighting against tremendous odds, being apprehended through the use of the despised "stool pigeon," and finally losing his battle to be subjected to punishment, suffering, and hardships, often awakens the sympathy of observers and leads them to entirely miss what is meant to be a deterrent influence.

Male, white, 23, sentenced for burglary, inmate of state reformatory.—The punishment given to criminals in such movies did not affect me that I remember, except for feeling sorry for the criminal—sometimes, and sometimes not.

Male, Negro, 24, sentenced for robbery, inmate of state reformatory.—In pictures I have seen, the law most always wins out in the end, but the bad guy is often the smartest guy, and the law gets wise through "stool pigeons," which makes one favor the bad guy. Every child likes a smart guy, no matter if he is a criminal or a cop.

Male, white, 19, sentenced for burglary, inmate of reformatory.—Best of all the movies I like city ones. I can understand them and feel at home. I don't like the endings of many of these for the gangster always reforms and gets married. Many of the shows have made me hate the copper. Most of the arrests they make in the pictures are false and they aren't made that way in real life. . . . I like crook pictures and admire the gang leader, not because I would want to be in his place, because I wouldn't want to, but he is interesting because he is different. There are always so many policemen against the crook and because he is alone, we like to see him get a break.

Male, white, 25, sentenced for robbery, ex-convict.—Now, I never go to shows. I did go to see the "Big House." It was the real thing. I'll bet every "hood" in Chi was down at M——— that week. I met about 10 guys I knew from the "joint." They ought to show that down there. I'll bet they'd tear the walls down. Boy, they were "crude." I'll bet everyone in the pen

[4] See also page 138.

could pull something like that, especially when they want "eats."
I know how them guys felt. They had the right idea "to kill or
get killed" and that is what is needed when anything like that
happens.

*Male, white, Jewish, 18, sentenced for robbery, rape, inmate of
state reformatory.*—I always feel like doing something wrong
after I see a gang picture, with the feeling that I can get away
with it. I think it is not right for the crook to be punished when
he is caught. I am always with the underdog regardless whether
he is right or wrong. I think the crook should be honored for
living the life of a criminal; for it sure takes courage every time
a thug does a crime. He is taking his life in his hands day and
night, for everyone is against him at all times.

8. *Feeling of resentment against punishment.*—The punishment of offenders in motion pictures may incite intense
resentment on the part of delinquent and criminal observers. Instead of a deterrent influence in such situations,
the person has distinctly hostile reactions to punishment
and to the agents who administer it. This resentment to
punishment portrayed in the movies and hostile reactions
to officers of the law can be frequently traced back to the
personal experience of the delinquent or criminal observers.
Disagreeable memories of their experiences and of officers
of the law with whom they have come in contact are called
forth.

Male, white, 26, sentenced for robbery, ex-convict.—The picture
"Hell's Gateway," was a good one, but the part where the coppers had Mileway and were giving him the "works"—they
would light a "smoke" and blow it into his face, eat candy and
sandwiches in front of him and mock him to have one. This is
cruel, but true. The coppers do worse than that. When I hear
or see a thing like that I'd like to have a machine gun and step
in and "mow" them down. It could be done. But you'd have
to have "guts"—it's a wonder some of the "Leggers" haven't
done it.

Male, white, 25, sentenced for burglary, ex-convict.—Yes, I resent society and I don't think I got a square deal. When I saw pictures of a prosecuting attorney giving a bitter fight to a jury, I thought of that——, that demanded I get two sentences to run consecutively. Right this minute if I saw him going down the street outside I think I'd attempt to kill him. He was a suave little Jew, that after each remark he made, he'd turn around and have a smirk on his face and look and see if the people in the courtroom was watching him. He was a "show-off" to the nth degree. I'd willingly hang, if I knew he was to die, also. God! I hate that guy. The only person I have ever hated in my life.

I remember the words he said to the judge as plain as if I had them written on paper:

> "Your Honor! According to law this man has committed burglary, but to my mind and yours he committed M-U-R-D-E-R!"

and he screamed that murder as though someone was trying to murder him.

Male, white, 23, rape, ex-convict.—Yes, I have always resented society. I thought it all out when I saw "The Trial of Mary Dugan." Some people think "Bum-raps" are something a bum does on your door when he knocks. They think coppers are priests, prosecuting attorneys are angels and judges the Disciples, but they are nothing but a bunch of gold-grabbing sons-of——. Why, Judge——, that lazy b——, was his mother's panderer. Square deal, why, what's the matter with them people you are working for? Are they crazy?

Male, white, 18, sentenced for burglary, inmate of reformatory.—I feel sorry for the fellow who gets captured in a crime picture. Most of them are. They do not keep right ahead because they think they can get away with it. . . . My feelings toward a burglar or gangster play are that I wish to see him escape safely. Not much unless it is true to life. Then I get excited over it much more. I feel rotten and plumb "booboo," because I hate to see him get sent up the river and not only that but I hold a grudge against the copper who sent him over. Most of the men and boys get a bum rap, and not only that but they are sent up the river to have them out of the way. Is it not true?

Male, white, sentenced for larceny, ex-convict.—When a fellow gets punished I resent it. I guess I just picture myself in his place. You remember how the fellows used to jeer and scrape their feet, and cough and get sort of stirred up when a picture like this was shown (in the penal institution), and when the scene showed a prisoner or a man getting tried, well, that only showed the uneasiness in their minds. I think all of the fellows thought about the same thing in a play like that.

E. SUMMARY

The materials which we have presented in this chapter make it clear that the deterrent influence of motion pictures on crime is not definite or consistent. If we rely upon the questionnaire responses of delinquents of both sexes, and of criminals, we see the admission by a substantial proportion that motion pictures may promote good conduct and discourage bad conduct. Yet there is much indication that these declarations refer to temporary effects. In addition there is considerable material showing how pictures supposedly exercising deterrent effects come to be discounted, ignored, and even reacted against in a hostile spirit. A short summary statement will help one to realize the inconsistency of the rôle of motion pictures as a deterrent agency.

The ways in which motion pictures seem to serve as a deterrent were found to be three: (1) playing upon the sentiments and arousing desires "to be good"; (2) showing delinquent or criminal conduct as unattractive and dangerous; (3) making a vivid portrayal of the punishment of the offenders. As over against this, we should notice the short life of the deterrent effect; the readiness to yield to temptation or to the injunctions of one's associates despite the movie experience (suggesting that the deterrent influence of motion pictures is not likely to be strong); the indifference to the punishment of the criminal as shown in motion pictures; the assertion by delinquents and criminals that motion pictures gloss over punishment as it is, and so do not make it vivid or keen; the tendency to discount pictures showing punishment of the criminal; the belief that one can outwit the law and thus escape punishment as it is shown; the sympathy for the criminal aroused by showing him being punished; and the feelings of resentment against society resulting from the punishment administered in the movies. Considerations such as these signify that the deterrent effects of motion pictures may be nullified, or that individuals may be immune to their influence.

We have not undertaken in this discussion any comparison of the conflicting tendencies which pictures may arouse. Consideration of this point is given elsewhere. Here it suffices to call attention to the inconsistent and indecisive character of motion pictures as an agency of deterring observers from engaging in delinquency or crime.

A few remarks might be made relative to the belief that a "moral" ending of a crime picture in which crime and wrongdoing are punished and virtue rewarded, overshadows other phases of the picture and leaves almost inevitable impressions of the futility of crime and the value of virtue. This notion regards the happy and moral climax in a picture as yielding the dominant impression, indeed, an impression which extends over all others and stamps them with its character. There is grave doubt whether this belief conforms to the experience of children and youths. From the accounts given in this chapter, elsewhere in this report, and in the volume *Movies and Conduct* it is evident that many fail to make an organized interpretation of a picture, centering around its ending. Indeed, nothing is clearer than the frequency with which details or elements of the picture may be picked out as dominantly significant to the exclusion or minimizing of the terminating episode. The child or adolescent seems ordinarily to have a wide range of scattered and unorganized interests, and, in addition, to be particularly responsive to incidents which are dramatic, exciting, and tempting. With this background, as our materials indicate, he is likely to approach motion pictures as a general source of life experience, responding to a variety of incidents that catch his attention, rather than to organize his reactions into a pattern dominated by the impression left by the ending climax of the picture. It would seem that many pictures conduce to this kind of experience by clothing questionable incidents with fascination and attractiveness, even though the ending, by implication, stamps them as wrong.

CHAPTER VII

MOTION PICTURES AND ATTITUDES TOWARDS CRIME

In this chapter we are presenting some material showing the influence of motion pictures in shaping attitudes on crime. We are particularly interested in indicating some conceptions of crime which seem to be formed by high-school students as a consequence of witnessing motion pictures. Subsequently some information will be given to show the judgments of criminals and prison wardens as to the effects of crime pictures.

A. ATTITUDES OF HIGH-SCHOOL STUDENTS

It seems quite clear from our material that the depiction of criminal activity in motion pictures has led some people to form a more tolerant and favorable attitude toward crime. On the other hand, movies have led others to condemn crime and have made them less tolerant of the criminal. These effects can be detected in the autobiographies written by high-school students. Many of them in their accounts indicate that pictures showing crime have made them sympathetic to the criminal and very frequently to the whole class of criminals. This expression of attitude does not mean that the high-school students who speak of it have been incited or tempted to engage in crime themselves (although there are some instances of this sort). It does signify, however, that they have developed certain conceptions of crime which make it more tolerated and of criminals which make them less reprehensible. Others make clear in their statements that the motion pictures have reënforced attitudes of condemnation towards crime or led them to be militant in their hostility to the criminal.

B. TOLERANT ATTITUDES TOWARDS CRIME

From the accounts which follow we can see that, as revealed by the experiences of high-school students, there are several ways by which motion pictures in treating crime may lead to a more tolerant attitude toward crime. To wit: pictures of criminal life may give the impression that hard work does not seem to pay; they may arouse sympathy for the criminal; they may seemingly justify the criminal act; they may portray the criminal as an attractive and fascinating character; they may portray the criminal act as romantic, adventuresome, and daring; they may show the criminal as a good samaritan aiding the weak and distressed; they may present crime as a benevolent enterprise of taking from the rich to help the poor. For purposes of convenient illustration we shall group the accounts given in this discussion under these seven heads.

1. Hard work does not seem to pay.
   Female, white, 17, high-school junior.—In one way the movies have made me feel more favorable towards crime. When one sees how the crooks make money by their bootlegging, etc., it seems hardly worthwhile for the plain business man to plod along year after year on a small salary.

   Female, white, 17, high-school junior.—When I see a movie where a man is a criminal and through circumstances comes out in the end a hero, it makes me feel that people who just go along minding their own business and striving to do what is right never get anywhere.

2. Sympathy for the criminal.

Female, white, 16, high-school junior.—The police chased a criminal who tried to reform after he finished his term at prison. The detectives were continually shadowing the poor fellow and my sympathy was entirely with him and his wife. His wife too aroused my sympathies because she would try to sidetrack the detectives in order to help her husband.

Female, white, 16, high-school sophomore.—Movies have made me less critical of criminals when I consider that all aren't as fortunate as we. Starvation has been the cause of more crime than anything else, as I see it in the movies. As a result I believe crime should be corrected instead of being punished, for the latter encourages more crime.

Female, white, 18, high-school junior.—In a sense, the movies have made me feel more favorable towards crime, especially by seeing a picture where one very dear member of a poor family is thrown in jail without any cause, while a rich person can get out free just by paying a large sum of money.

Female, white, 14, high-school sophomore.—Pictures and books have equally made me more broadminded. Usually crime pictures make me feel sorry for the criminals because the criminals probably didn't get the right start.

Female, white, 16, high-school junior.—I believe I feel more favorable to crime since I have seen the "Lone Wolf's Daughter." It showed the life of a reformed criminal and though not all criminals reform I believe that a number would if they had a chance.

3. Justifying the criminal act.

Female, white, 14, high-school sophomore.—From movies about crime I have never wanted to become a criminal and have always sided with the police in movie crimes. Nevertheless I have felt more favorable towards a movie criminal and a real criminal when I have seen that he had no other way but to commit the crime.

Female, Negro, 15, high-school junior.—Crime pictures I am not especially fond of. I think that people who disobey the law get their faults from their predecessors and one hardly finds a person of this type who has left a good home in order to engage in crime. In "The Noose" Richard Barthelmess, I think, was not to blame for the crimes that he committed, but that crime was forced into his head because his father was the gang-leader of that time.

Female, white, Mexican, 15, high-school freshman.—I saw a picture; it was called "Jesse James." This man was called a thief. I have seen where men are branded as hunted outlaws for killing someone, but when you find out their story they are either innocent or have killed in self-defense. That shows how you can always misjudge a person, and we should look on both sides of a thing before we decide.

Male, white, 16, high-school junior.—I think a lot of crime movies I have seen have made me feel more favorable towards crime by depicting the criminal as a hero who dies protecting his best friend against the police, or some movies show them as a debonair gentleman who robs at will from the rich and spares the poor. I have thought I would like to be a Robin Hood.

4. Portraying the criminal as an attractive and fascinating character.

Female, white, 16, high-school sophomore.—I always had the feeling that every criminal was wicked and there wasn't the slightest thing nice or kind about them. But since I have been seeing more pictures my ideas have changed, especially since I saw "Alias Jimmy Valentine."

Female, white, 18, high-school junior.—I think the movies have made me feel more favorable toward crime, although I've never had any ambition to engage in a criminal act. By crime I do not mean the brutal kind; that's out. But I do mean the crimes like "Alias Jimmy Valentine" and "The Underworld."

Female, white, 16, high-school sophomore.—Yes I sort of think movies have made me more favorable toward crime, especially "State Street Sadie." I was just mad about the criminal in that picture. Some time afterward, I met a man who was somewhat like him, and this of course attracted me to him. Some weeks later, he was arrested for smuggling guns in over the Mexican border.

5. Portrayal of the criminal act as romantic, daring, and adventuresome.

Female, Negro, 20, high-school senior.—The movies have painted crime very clear to me and as a result of seeing it as the movies depict it, it does not seem as bad sometimes as it really is. If the movie shows a play of crime and there is a very desperate crook who wears about two or three guns and can kill a man before he can even get his gun out and then fights it out with the cops and gets free, we all no doubt leave the theater admiring this crook. I have often done this but I never wanted to be a crook.

Female, white, 15, high-school junior.—Many times when I see pictures of the underworld and pictures of crime I kind of like men that do such things, but in real life I would certainly change my mind. I can't say that I have ever wanted to be a criminal but still I admire such parts in the pictures.

6. Picturing the criminal as a benevolent person.

Male, white, 16, high-school junior.—Yes, many times o'er I've desired to become a crook—and my ideal is Rob Roy, Scotland's greatest honorable crook, with Robin Hood close behind him.

Male, white, 14, high-school freshman.—When I saw "Robin Hood," "Don Q," and "The Thief of Bagdad," I felt very much like being a crook.

Female, white, 16, high-school sophomore.—Towards the kind of crime motion pictures nearly always depict, that is the chivalrous criminal—Robin Hood, for instance—I feel lenient. The real sordidness of crime is hardly ever displayed.

Female, white, 15, high-school sophomore.—"Alias Jimmy Valentine" made me feel more favorable toward crime. Yes, I had the desire to become benevolent criminal.

Female, white, 15, high-school sophomore.—In thinking of Robin Hood now I am put in a more joyful frame of mind and I will say that I have always felt that being a character like Robin Hood would be *the* life.

Male, white, 15, high-school freshman.—I would not mind being a benevolent criminal, but just to take the food and money and pass it around would be no fun. I would like to own a large building and have trapdoors in it and stairways that no one knew about but myself. Have a large landing field in it, have a cavern that was impossible to find. I would like to drop off and take something and have the cops chase me, head for a straight road and disappear from sight.

7. Picturing crime as a benevolent enterprise for the benefit of the poor.

Male, white, Jewish, 14, high-school freshman.—When I saw the picture "In Old Arizona," it made me feel that it would be good to be a criminal, as the one in the picture. It showed how he robbed the stagecoach and then took a pin off a lady. She asked him if he would steal from her. He then said, No, my dear lady, I do not steal from the individual. He said this all in a foreign voice. He then gave her gold worth twice as much as the pin was worth, and the lady thanked him very much. I think he was in some respects like Robin Hood, stealing from the big rich people and giving to the poor.

Female, white, 17, high-school junior.—Some movies have made me feel favorable toward crimes, especially that in which the crook does something to help those who need it. I think when the poor are weak and need money some one should be kind enough and generous to help them although "God helps those that help themselves."

Male, white, Jewish, 15, high-school freshman.—I had the desire to become a benevolent criminal like Robin Hood, because he helped the poor by stealing from the rich.

Female, Negro, 16, high-school junior.—In a great many movies of crime I've been led to respect a certain type of crook. The cheap and the high class. Of course, both are dangerous, but you can hardly have as much respect for one who preys on those beneath him as you would for one who picks on the "big fellow."

Male, white, Jewish, 16, high-school sophomore.—Sometimes I think being a criminal like Robin Hood would not be a crime. Taking rich men's money who have gotten their money illegitimately and giving it to the poor and needy would seem all right.

Male, white, Jewish, 16, high-school sophomore.—Robin Hood has been my favorite for a long time. A burglar never seemed more benevolent than him. I was thrilled watching him robbing the rich and helping the poor. Warner Baxter nearly duplicated this in "Old Arizona."

Male, white, Lithuanian, 19, high-school junior.—Movies have made me want to become a benevolent criminal like Robin Hood. This happened after I saw "Robin Hood"; I wanted to help the poor. This is partly due to the fact that I lived in a poor neighborhood and have seen those people, mostly the women, slave and work the whole day and part of the night trying to clothe the young ones while the father is out drinking and never brings home his pay. These facts I have seen.

Female, Negro, 19, high-school senior.—I can't say that movies have made me more favorable toward crime. I was getting to think that there was crime committed which was perfect until I saw "The Perfect Crime." I wished that I could be an honorable criminal like Robin Hood or Jimmie Dale who helped the poor and robbed the rich.

It is necessary to be cautious in interpreting the accounts which have been presented. They do not say that motion pictures have incited to crime those who have written the accounts. They do show, however, that motion pictures may lead some people to a more tolerant attitude toward crime and toward the criminal, and they suggest the ways in which this may be done. It is not contended, of course, that the particular view of crime or of the criminal which is developed in any one of these ways becomes the exact conception which the individual forms of crime or of criminals. Merely to see, and to be attracted toward, a Robin Hood in motion pictures does not mean that one conceives all criminals as courageous and honorable persons, or all crime as a worthy enterprise for the benefit of the poor or distressed. And similarly with the other ways we have illustrated. Yet it should be apparent that views of particu-

lar types of crime and criminals, such as have been formed
by the writers of the accounts given, do exert some influence
on the general stereotyped conceptions of crime and criminals.
Many of the writers of the accounts admit this to be true.

It is now proper to give what statistical information we
have on the extent to which motion pictures induce this
more favorable and tolerant attitude toward crime. Of a
sample of 203 autobiographies of high-school boys 18 per
cent indicated that the motion pictures made them favorable to crime or the criminal. Forty-two per cent indicated
that the motion pictures did not arouse attitudes favorable
to crime, while 40 per cent did not write on this topic. Of
the 121 boys who discussed this problem 29 per cent revealed
that motion pictures created favorable attitudes toward
crime, while 71 per cent indicated that this was not the
case. Of a sample of 255 autobiographies of high-school
girls 11 per cent indicated that motion pictures instilled
attitudes favorable to crime; 40 per cent indicated that
motion pictures did not arouse favorable attitudes toward
crime; while 49 per cent did not write on the problem. Of
the 131 girls who wrote on the topic 21 per cent showed
clearly that motion pictures aroused attitudes favorable
toward crime or the criminal, while 79 per cent were not
influenced in this way. Thus, it is evident that, roughly, one
fourth of the students who wrote about this item speak of
forming attitudes favorable toward crime or the criminal
as a result of motion pictures, the percentage being somewhat higher for boys than for girls.

C. Condemnation of Crime

One can easily see from the statistical information which
has been given that many report not to have been more
favorably disposed by motion pictures toward crime. Many,

indeed, declare that motion pictures have made them less tolerant of crime. There recurs in their statements the theme, "crime does not pay."

Male, Negro, 14, high-school senior.—The moving pictures have never made me favor crime. In fact, they have prejudiced me against it. I have never cared for pictures dealing with the underworld, and gang wars, and I have never in all my life wanted to become any kind of a criminal. I loathe the very idea of a life of crime for myself or for any of my associates. Movies have developed no desire in me for the things of the lower elements; rather they have turned me against crime forever.

Female, white, 16, high-school sophomore.—The movies did not make me more favorable to crime. I think they made me go against crime. The movies gave me the idea that crime doesn't pay, for you never get away with it. The movies taught me many other valuable things.

Male, white, 17, high-school senior.—Crime pictures have inspired in me not the ambition to be a criminal, but to be something in this world that would enable me to help decrease the presence of that degraded occupation. After seeing many crime pictures I have come to a conclusion that crime does not pay. Many people say that criminal pictures are an incentive to crime, that they urge upon the younger generation the benefits of crime. However, I think the contrary is true. Criminal pictures usually end in the death or imprisonment of the criminal.

Male, Negro, 16, high-school freshman.—I have not yet seen a picture that would make me feel favorably toward crime because the criminals suffer sooner or later. I hope to never be a criminal of any kind because I have respect for my parents.

Female, white, 15, high-school junior.—The movies have shown how seemingly easy it is to commit a crime and how easy it is to yield to temptation. On the other hand, they have shown the consequences. I have had minor temptations but I have quickly dismissed them from my mind because I knew there would be consequences. I have never been favorable towards crime.

Male, white, Italian, 15, high-school freshman.—Movies made me strong against all sorts of crime. It made me hate crime worse than ever. I've always wished that crime would be wiped out, but have realized that as long as there is man, there is crime. Although now I go to see murder stories and enjoy them, there is never a thought in my head which makes me want to become a criminal. It would sooner make me want to become a detective.

Male, white, 17, high-school junior.—Movies have not made me favorable toward crime. It has done just the opposite. As for a desire to engage in crime—I have never felt that. I remember seeing the picture, "Robin Hood," in which Douglas Fairbanks starred. Even my favorite actor could not change me. I do not profess to be perfect in any way, but I have never felt favorable towards crime, and I do not think the movies will change my opinion.

One can see from these accounts that the fashioning of attitudes on crime by motion pictures is in no sense merely along one direction. In fact, in this area of experience, as in the case of others, the influence of motion pictures is quite paradoxical. Some people are influenced along one direction, others along a different direction. In some sense, it is hardly to be expected that the effects of motion pictures would be consistently in one direction.[1] That the treatment of crime in motion pictures should make people both more tolerant of crime and more set against it is not unexpected, even though it appear contradictory.

It is assumed that the development of attitudes by motion pictures against crime constitutes no problem of public concern. The recognition of this one direction of influence should not obscure the fact that motion pictures may work in the opposite direction, making people more charitable and lenient in their attitudes toward crime. We have sought to present the evidence on this point yielded by our materials.

[1] See the chapter on "Social Milieu and Motion Picture Influence" for a discussion of this matter.

D. ATTITUDES OF CRIMINALS

Criminals, themselves, frequently assert that motion pictures are apt to influence young boys and girls to lives of delinquency and crime, even when they claim that they themselves have not been influenced in this way. One inmate of a penal institution writes with considerable insight on this point, as follows:

Male, white, 21, sentenced for robbery, inmate of reformatory.— Many of the gangster pictures don't show much about the punishment of the crook if he's caught. They don't show much of the prison he's sent to and the bad parts of the jail life; instead they show a picture every now and then of the prison office and the walls when he goes to prison and when he goes out. They should show the public more of the prison tortures a criminal gets if he should happen to disobey a small rule of the prison, or mention the many lonely nights he has to spend for his crime, and all his disappointments.

The pictures don't show all the marks of a prison; instead they show the easy life the crook leads and how he spends the "Hog Money" on women and booze and how he beats all the raps which are against him if he ever gets caught. Such boloney should be cut out of pictures or else not let any kids see the shows.

Things the shows should not picture are the easy ways of a crook and how he holds up a big payroll or blows open a safe in the middle of the night. The cabarets and all of the open gambling dens. The underworld and all of its gang wars and many other things which influence the mind of a boy who lives in a shabby neighborhood where such gangs organize together. The adventure and excitement is partly the fault of gangster pictures that influence boys who go with small gangs already. They see a burglar in a show break into a store and get away and that probably makes them try the same and see if their luck's as good as the next one; if they succeed the first time, nine chances out of ten they'll try it again, if they're a bunch of fools which most crooks are. They keep trying it till they get arrested and then it's too late to be sorry then and probably go to a small institution where they get a little more knowledge from more experienced fellows.

It is interesting to observe that 62 per cent of the group of 110 male reformatory inmates, used as a sample in this study, expressed their belief that the witnessing of gangster and burglar pictures is likely to lead boys or young men into crime. Twenty-six per cent stated that they did not feel this to be true; 12 per cent expressed no judgment. The proportion who believe that motion pictures have this effect always exceeds by far those who admit that motion pictures have had that effect on themselves.

E. ATTITUDES OF PRISON WARDENS

Of a sample of 122 heads of penal and correctional institutions, 58, or 48 per cent, felt that the ordinary run of movies shown to boys and girls and youths and young women are likely to lead some of them to lives of delinquency and crime; 31, or 25 per cent, felt that they were not likely to; while 33, or 27 per cent, did not express an opinion. It is interesting to note the responses of those who expressed the affirmative belief when asked to explain why they regarded movies as likely to have this effect. Most typical of the answers which were given are the following:

"False conceptions of life are shown in motion pictures."
"Crime and delinquency are glorified."
"Disrespect for law is created."
"Motion pictures suggest unlawful acts to boys at impressionable ages."
"Many movies are not of character-building type."
"Individuals with poor or unbalanced minds are led astray by motion pictures."
"Motion pictures suggest crimes previously unthought-of."
"Sensational life, not real life, is shown."

We are making no evaluation of the judgments of these prison wardens or heads of correctional institutions.

F. Summary

In this chapter we have sought to present briefly two sets of material: (1) the attitudes of high-school students towards crime and criminals as influenced by the movies; and (2) the judgments of criminals and heads of prison and correctional schools on whether motion pictures lead boys and young men to crime.

As we have tried to show, it seems clear from the expressions of experience given by high-school students that motion pictures have led many of them to a more lenient and tolerant view of crime and criminals. It is also clear that many of these students have been influenced in the opposite way by motion pictures. This contradiction in effect, while it seems to confuse the situation, is not unexpected. People may be influenced in different ways by the same pictures.

The criminals and the penal heads who have given us their judgments attach much importance to the influence of motion pictures in leading youths to crime. To what extent these judgments arise out of personal observations (both groups seem to be in a strategic position to make observations) or merely reflect public stereotypes on the influence of motion pictures we are not in a position to judge.

CHAPTER VIII

THE SOCIAL MILIEU AND MOTION-PICTURE INFLUENCE

ALTHOUGH, as we have shown in previous chapters, motion pictures influence some people in several ways, nevertheless not all observers of given motion pictures are affected alike. We may very well ask why different groups of people are influenced differently by the same pictures; also what people seem to be subject most to influence by the movies.

Two important points are to be noted: first, the content of motion pictures is diverse and, frequently, conflicting in character; second, people come to the motion pictures from different social backgrounds and consequently are likely to have different attitudes and interests. The second point is especially significant, for attitudes acquired prior to motion-picture experience influence the selection and interpretation of what is seen.

A. VARIETY AND CONFLICT IN THEMES DEALT WITH IN MOTION PICTURES

One can detect in the kinds of pictures that we have been considering ideas which in relation to one another are frequently confusing and sometimes conflicting. The same picture may frequently present a form of life as something attractive and alluring, and yet imply that it is something that is dishonorable and to be condemned. For example, many pictures treating crime are likely to play up luxury, ease, power, and popularity, suggesting incidentally that they may be attained easily by questionable means, yet at the same time they may end by depicting the ultimate misfortune or ill fate of the criminal. The presentation, in other words, is not likely to induce a clean-cut reaction upon the part of the observer. It may instead release a variety of motives which are frequently confusing and sometimes conflicting. A boy may be distinctly attracted and stirred up by the adventure, power, and wealth of the criminal career shown, yet also be apprehensive as to the fate of one who undertakes crime. This is mentioned merely as an example of the lack of consistency in the theme of a picture. In general, it is true that motion pictures present a variety of themes and forms of life, which call forth, and play upon, a corresponding variety of motives and attitudes.

We are presenting a few autobiographical accounts which reflect this multiplicity of patterns of life seen in motion pictures.

Male, white, 16, high-school sophomore.—Movies made me feel for another life than that of our neighborhood. Many times I wished to be a cowboy, or trapper, or jungle hunter, yearning for the adventurous lives of those men as shown in the movies. Sometimes I wish to be a soldier fighting and winning as in the movies, or a general commanding and charging against the enemies. Sometimes I was wondering about slipping into a rich building and walking out with valuables as in the movies. But most times, to be a criminal made me feel such men ought to be caught and given life in jail. After seeing or reading about Robin Hood, I wished I would be as famous as him and experience the same adventures.

Male, Negro, 17, high-school junior.—Well, sometimes I would have several daydreams, but one would always stand out above the others. For instance, I would sometimes dream that I was rich or wealthy and would have plenty of money or even a rich mansion and automobile in which wealthy people ride. I would sometimes be tempted to act like some of the movie stars I had seen. Then again I would like to be like some crook who I have seen in some underworld plays, such as ——————— in the ———————. There were, of course, many temptations I have had in seeing a number of these pictures.

Male, Negro, 14, high-school freshman.—Cowboy pictures, war pictures, fighting (boxing) pictures, and underworld pictures give me new ambitions. I want to be like the star of any of these pictures. Sometimes I would imagine myself being a great gunman. Then whenever a policeman was the star of an underworld picture, I would want to become a great detective. Whenever I saw a boxing picture I would desire to become the greatest fighter that ever lived or would be born. War pictures gave me ambition to be a soldier. I wanted to fly a plane. I daydreamed of becoming the world's foremost flyer, but the sight of another picture would change my ambition. Sometimes the movies gave me a desire to become rich. I would daydream of being many times the richest man in the world. I wanted to make all my relatives and the poor people rich.

Male, white, 15, high-school sophomore.—Sometimes movies make me think of myself as a criminal. I think of all the good times I could have with the money. I think of spending my proceeds of a criminal venture in an amusement park, at parties, in night clubs. Then my thought takes a different trend and I think that free spending of money and not working during the day might make the police suspicious. I then think of saving all the stolen money and working at day time so the police wouldn't be suspicious of me. Again I think that it wouldn't be fun robbing poor people like it sometimes shows in the movies because they work hard for their money. I then think of robbing rich people, but I think again that after all they work for their money also. The plan that springs into my mind is that of robbing a gambling establishment. If I succeeded the head of the establishment would not and could not tell the police because they would arrest him for operating a gambling den. I would then give part of the money to poor people and part of it I would keep for myself. But at the end of my thoughts I realize that no matter how skillful he may be or how clever he may be or how much protection he has the crook is always caught sometime or other. If he isn't caught he is killed by one of his associates. So I think that after all I might as well remain honest, try to make money in an honest way and spend it if and when I want to without the fear of being arrested or killed.

Male, white, Italian, 13, high-rate delinquency area.—When I see a gangster picture I want to be one and carry a gun. It makes you feel like you'd like to walk the streets at midnight and bump off a guy. It actually makes you feel tougher. I've felt that way plenty of times. Sometimes I've seen pictures that have made me want to rob. Most of them make you feel that if you rob you'll get caught some day. ——————————— made me feel that way. I learned how to bump off a guy. A guy used to come out of a railroad with plenty of money. The two guys came up to the guy and asked him what time it was, then he said, "stick 'em up." . . . I've seen plenty of pictures that made me feel like I'd like to go straight. Some crime pictures make me feel like I'd like to be the good guy.

B. BACKGROUND OF EXPERIENCE

Alongside of the diversity of content of motion pictures we may set the variety of interests and desires of different groups of movie-goers. The backgrounds of experience of people vary and accordingly result in different lines of interest. The early experiences of the child serve as the basis for his future experiences, sensitizing him to some influences and immunizing him to others.

We may notice this condition in comparing the rôle of motion pictures in the lives of boys who live in widely different communities. The child reared in a high-rate delinquency area may acquire attitudes which make him more receptive to the portrayal on the screen of delinquent or criminal forms of behavior, while the child reared in a low-rate delinquency area tends to be impervious to them. The autobiographical material presented for purposes of convenience under the headings "Sensitivity to Crime" and "Immunization to Crime" makes this quite clear.

The first series are accounts given in interviews by several Italian boys living in a disorganized area in Chicago having the second highest rate of delinquency in the city.

Sensitized to Crime in Motion Pictures

Male, white, Italian, 14, high-rate delinquency area.—"When I was 9 de gang of guys I played wit began to make clubs. We made one in ————'s yard. We used to go to radio stores and get big boxes and fix em up like houses and cover dem wit tar paper and oil cloth. We chipped in a nickle a week and at de end of de week we used to have a party. If we didn't have a nickle we used to have to pay a nickle extra de next week. Dere was a bakery store across de street and we used to buy stale bread for a nickle. We used to get nuts too and pick em out. We used to get junk and sell it and keep the money in a little box in de club. We used to tell stories in de club when it was dark, den we'd get scared and go home. De biggest boy was de leader of de club. When I was ten years old I moved to where I live now. My ma thought I'd learn more at a Catholic school. I didn't like de sisters; one of dem hit me when I didn't do nottin, and I didn't like her. I went bummin for two weeks. It was in de winter and I used to hang around in de halls and den I started to ride on an "American" newspaper truck.

"Den I started to ——— School. I got along all right, but den I met a big guy dat was just out of parental school. We planned on running away. We hiked and asked for lifts until we got to K———. We stole an old Ford dere and we got caught. De big guy saw a Ford in a field. He said, "Let's take it and drive to Chi and take a good car and come back. We went about ten miles and a cop in a car hands us up and took us to a station. He pulled his gun on de big guy. I was scared den. Dey searched us and dey took a knife off a' de middle-sized guy. Dey kept us in jail and our parents came and got us. My fadder didn't whip me; he just asked me if I wasn't ashamed of myself.

"I liked de guy ———————— dat was ————————. He always acted nice in crook pictures; he was a tough guy. I liked him because he was small and could go out and kill people and take dere money; and he could blow up safes and get de dough. I used to go wit odder guys and we felt dat we'd like to be like him and rob stores and tings.

"I didn't like love pictures. De gang never liked dem kind of shows. We used to sneak in at times.

"I never stole anything till I got to dis neighborhood. It was after I moved to dis neighborhood dat I began to like crook pictures. Den I started stealing stuff at de market and taking tings."

Male, white, Italian, 13, high-rate delinquency area.—"We liked gangster pictures. We'd talk about it; we'd say dey make money easy and do you tink we could make money easy like dat. I never had an idea of being a gangster but I wished I could be. I used to act like a gangster. I'd put a cigarette in my mouth and act tough.

"Den L—— told us it was easy. We wouldn't get caught. He said we'd have lots of money and could go to shows and buy things and wouldn't have to be dependent on anybody for money. I wouldn't go because I was afraid. But he called me yellow and so I went. We'd divide de gang; some would go one night and some would go another night. The first night I went we made eight stores; we got $3.75 a piece. There were three of us. After dat I felt it was safe; dat dey wouldn't have an idea that any of us kids would do dat.

"We used to feel like big shots den. We used to tell de kids you work all week and we only pull one job and make as much as you do. We tought we were tough guys around our house. When we got caught, I felt punk. I said to myself I aint going any more, dat it don't pay. After dat de gang broke up."

Immunization to Crime

The following accounts are from a number of high-school students living in stable communities (Chicago) where the rate of delinquency is low and patterns of crime unfamiliar.

They will give an idea of how such a background of experience may bulwark the individual against any appeal or attraction of crime.

Male, Negro, 15, high-school sophomore.—There is, as I can remember, only one type of picture that makes me feel prejudiced and they are crime pictures. I have been prejudiced against crime and criminals from early boyhood—and intend to be until death.

Male, 17, white, high-school sophomore.—I have often wished that there were no crooks. I like to see crime movies but I never sympathize with the criminal. I wish that every criminal was dead. They are only a menace to the public and often lead other people into trouble who would not otherwise become a crook.

Male, 15, white, Jewish, high-school sophomore.—Movies have reinforced my opinion of crime and made me feel more averse to crime than ever. Many movies give a good picture of real criminals and the crimes they commit and sometimes I feel like becoming the Mayor of the City and abolishing crime by my own means since there is no need for crooked politics and the men in office take bribes from the criminals.

Male, 17, white, high-school junior.—And these crime pictures portraying the thief as a man who is good and just and only trying to support his aged mother! The writers ought to be shot for such stuff. Instead of showing that crime is all wrong from any viewpoint, the picture usually tries to defend the thief. And about this "no children admitted" type of picture. That such vile stuff can be shown on the screen in front of gaping crowds and then called "swell stuff" is a mighty wonder to me. That's my view of pictures in general and I will stick to it until better pictures are shown.

Female, white, Jewish, 14, high-school freshman.—The pictures I hate to see are gangster and underworld pictures. I also hate to see pictures of night clubs. One of the pictures which I did enjoy was "Queen of the Night Club." It was about gangsters and how a man shot another man and when the police came he hid in the davenport. No picture ever made me feel favorable towards crime. My mother taught me since I was a child never to steal or do anything like that and if I would see gold before me and it is not mine I would not touch it.

Female, white, 17, high-school junior.—Our family is so against evil and crime that I have become so versed in the feeling that no matter what the feeling of an individual may be I believe he or she should better control his emotions than to commit any sort of crime. As for me, I do not consider any sort of crime honorable.

In presenting these two series of accounts, there is no intention of implying that all individuals who live in areas where delinquency is a familiar pattern will derive from crime pictures incentive to delinquency, nor that, conversely, all living in communities where there is little or no delinquency are immunized to any attraction of such pictures. In general, however, this difference in community experience will dispose the individuals to different interpretations of what is seen and to make different selections from it.

Some further realization of the significance of social and community backgrounds in sensitizing individuals differently to motion pictures should come from certain findings gained from the questionnaire given to the grade-school children living in markedly different areas of Chicago.

Boys and girls living in the high-, medium-, and low-rate delinquency areas were asked to rank in order of their preference the following kinds of pictures: cowboy; airplane; love; detective; "spooky"; news reels; serials; gangster. The ranking of gangster and airplane pictures tends to suggest area differences rather clearly. Eleven per cent of the boys in the high-rate delinquency areas ranked gangster pictures as first in order of their preference; while this was done by only 6 per cent of the boys in the medium-rate delinquency areas and 4 per cent in the low-rate delinquency areas. The boys in a truant and behavior-problem school agreed, interestingly enough, with the boys in the high-rate delinquency areas, 11 per cent of them ranking gangster pictures as their first choice. In indicating preference for airplane pictures a reversal is discernible. Twenty-one per cent of the boys in the truant and behavior-problem school and 20 per cent of the boys in the high-rate delinquency areas selected this type of picture as their first choice, whereas 33 per cent of the boys in the medium-rate delinquency areas and 47 per cent in the low-rate delinquency areas indicated airplane pictures as first choice.

The influence of the social world of the individual resulting in motion-picture preferences is even more strikingly revealed in sex differences. Only 1 per cent, 2 per cent, and none of the girls in the high-, medium-, and low-rate delinquency areas, respectively, as contrasted with 11 per cent, 6 per cent, and 4 per cent of the boys in the respective areas indicated gangster pictures as first choice. On the other hand, where only 3 per cent, 6 per cent, and 1 per cent of the boys in the respective areas preferred love pictures as their first choice, 32 per cent, 26 per cent, and 24 per cent of the girls in these areas ranked love pictures first in order of preference. It is to be noted that the girls in the high-rate delinquency areas have the greatest preference for love pictures, while the girls in the medium- and low-rate delinquency areas follow in order. This seems to reflect again differences in the social worlds of the girls in these different areas.

To the question, "Which of the following kinds [1] of life do the movies usually show in an interesting way?", 45 per cent of the truant and behavior-problem boys, 28 per cent of the high-rate delinquency area boys, 21 per cent of the medium-rate delinquency area boys, and 21 per cent of the

[1] College life, home life, life of the criminal, wealthy or rich life, honest life, hard work, fighting, having a good time.

low-rate delinquency area boys indicated the life of the criminal. A sex difference can also be observed in this response; only 9 per cent of the girls in the high-rate delinquency areas, 6 per cent in the medium-rate delinquency areas, and 9 per cent in the low-rate delinquency areas indicated that the life of the criminal is portrayed by the movies in an interesting way.

Sex differences can be observed also in the responses to the question "Is fighting usually portrayed in an interesting way in the movies?" Forty-one per cent of the truant and behavior-problem boys, 36 per cent in the high-rate delinquency areas, 33 per cent in the medium-rate delinquency areas, and 33 per cent in the low-rate delinquency areas answered in the affirmative; whereas only 14, 10, and 9 per cent of the girls in these respective delinquency areas indicated that fighting is usually shown in an interesting way on the screen.

Interesting area differences also are suggested in response to the question, "Have you seen any pictures which made you want to be real good?" Sixty per cent of the truant and behavior-problem boys, 72 per cent of the boys in the high-rate delinquency area, 56 per cent of those in the medium-rate delinquency areas, and 53 per cent in the low-rate delinquency areas indicated that some pictures make them want to be "real good." The same trend is evident in the responses of the girls, 77 per cent in the high-rate delinquency areas, 64 per cent in the medium-rate delinquency areas, and 40 per cent in the low-rate delinquency areas indicating the same influence.[2]

Area and sex differences are evident in the case of other

[2] The larger response to this question on the part of those living in areas of high delinquency is interesting, but not unexpected. Because of the disintegration of their codes, with greater temptations, and greater indulgence in bad or questionable conduct, there is more occasion for feeling that one is "bad" and so a likelihood for a greater number to feel the temporary attraction "to be good."

items of motion-picture influence. Forty-five per cent of the truant and behavior-problem boys and 39 per cent of the boys in the high-rate delinquency areas indicated that motion pictures made them want to make a lot of money easily, whereas 20 per cent of the boys in the medium-rate delinquency areas and 19 per cent of the boys in the low-rate delinquency areas indicated a similar influence. When asked what kinds of pictures made them want to make a lot of money easily, 35 per cent of the truant and behavior-problem boys, 34 per cent of the boys in the high-rate delinquency areas, 20 per cent of the boys in the medium-rate delinquency areas, and 17 per cent of the boys in the low-rate delinquency areas indicated, in free response, that pictures of the gangster, fighting, and gun-play type so affected them.

Among the girls, 35 per cent in the high-rate delinquency areas stated that movies made them want to make a lot of money easily, whereas 16 per cent of the girls in the medium-rate delinquency areas, and 14 per cent in the low-rate delinquency areas indicated a similar influence. When asked to respond freely to the question "What types of pictures aroused such desires?" 14 per cent of the girls in the high-rate delinquency areas, 5 per cent in the medium-rate delinquency areas, and 1 per cent in the low-rate delinquency areas indicated "fast life, sex pictures."

It is strongly suggested in these questionnaire responses that residence in different communities, implying significant differences in experiences and associates, reflects itself in a different sensitivity to motion pictures. One can trace, usually, a definite trend in this sensitivity in passing from a disorganized, high-rate delinquency area, through a medium-rate delinquency area, to an area where the rate of delinquency is low.

C. CONCLUSION

The materials presented in this chapter and in previous chapters seem to throw some light on the two questions "Why are different groups affected by motion pictures differently?" and "What portion of the population seems to be most subject to influence by the movies?" It seems quite clear that the variety of influences which motion pictures may exercise arises from the wide range of themes and patterns of conduct which are shown, and the different backgrounds of experience of the observers. Because of their difference in experience, gained mainly from the groups in which they live, persons acquire attitudes which sensitize or immunize them to certain motion picture influences. The likelihood is for boys and girls reared in low-rate delinquency areas to be less susceptible to questionable patterns of conduct shown on the screen.

It should be noted as a further point that children living in high-rate delinquency areas have more opportunity and greater temptations to engage in delinquency than children in better socially organized areas. Motion pictures may excite in boys in both areas thoughts and desires conducive to delinquency, yet the boys in the stable, well-organized community may not engage in delinquency, while those in the area of social disorganization may do so.

From our materials it would seem that persons living in high-rate delinquency areas are most subject to influence by the themes of life treated by motion pictures. In these areas of high social disorganization [3] the family and school and church play a relatively minor rôle in the life of the child. Parents in all areas may be equally aware of possible dire consequences of some motion pictures, as is indicated

[3] See Shaw's *Delinquency Areas* and Burgess' "The Growth of the City," in Park and Burgess' *The City*.

by the fact that in response to the question, "Do your parents tell you some movies are bad?" 76 per cent of the truant and behavior-problem boys, 75 per cent of the high-rate delinquency area boys, 79 per cent of the medium-rate delinquency area boys, and 76 per cent of the low-rate delinquency area boys responded in the affirmative.   In the areas of high delinquency and social disorganization, however, the parents as a rule tend to lose control over their children, as a result, apparently, of culture conflicts.[4]   In this situation motion pictures assume more importance as an educational agency for the boy and girl, and become a·significant source of many ideas and schemes of life.   It is to be expected perhaps that truant and behavior-problem boys and, in general, boys and girls in areas of high delinquency, would be influenced more by motion pictures, towards delinquency, than would boys living in stable areas of little delinquency.

The influence of motion pictures on the behavior of individuals may be regarded against the background of other institutions.   The community and groups of which the child is a part transmit to him tradition and custom, forms of thought and behavior.   Especially important in transmitting this social heritage have been the family, the school, the neighborhood, and the church.   In recent years motion pictures seem to have become an important agency in transmitting patterns of thought and behavior.[5]   Yet peculiarly the influence that they exert in this respect seems to be in inverse proportion to the strength of family and neighborhood, school and church.   Where these traditional institutions are relatively highly organized, motion pictures are seemingly of lesser influence, though nevertheless a factor in forming social attitudes and transmitting schemes of life.

[4] See Louis Wirth, "Culture Conflict and Misconduct," *Journal of Social Forces*, June, 1931.
[5] See *Movies and Conduct*.

CHAPTER IX

MOTION PICTURES IN CORRECTIONAL AND PENAL INSTITUTIONS

THE showing of motion pictures in correctional schools and penal institutions has gained in popularity in recent years. In a sample of 109 penitentiaries and reformatories studied by the National Society for Penal Information [1] motion pictures were portrayed in 85 institutions to 90,-931 prisoners out of a total of 114,248. Assuming that the same proportions hold for correctional and penal institutions not included in this survey, about 80 per cent of the prison population in the United States have the opportunity to observe motion pictures during their period of incarceration. In connection with our study it seemed fruitful to inquire into the effects of motion pictures shown in penal institutions.

Questions that immediately suggest themselves are: How frequently are motion pictures shown? How and by whom are they selected? What types of pictures are shown? Table 1 summarizes the situation in 1929 as regards frequency with which motion pictures are presented.

Twenty-three, or 24 per cent, of a sample of 96 institutional heads stated that they would show movies more frequently if they could; while 68, or 71 per cent, stated they would not, and 5, or 5 per cent, did not answer the question. Of a sample of 26 heads of institutions where motion pictures are not shown 85 per cent indicated they would show them if they could, most of them being prevented from doing so by lack of facilities or apparatus.

[1] *American Prisons and Reformatories. 1929 Handbook.*

TABLE 1

SUMMARY OF FREQUENCY OF MOTION PICTURES SHOWN IN STATE AND FEDERAL PRISONS IN THE UNITED STATES

(Compiled from *American Prisons and Reformatories, 1929 Handbook*, The National Society of Penal Information.)

Frequency Shown	Number of Prisoners		Number of Prisons	
	Number	Per Cent	Number	Per Cent
Movies shown during entire year				
7 per week	1,708	1.9	1	1.2
4 " "	207	.2	1	1.2
3 " "	852	.9	3	3.5
2 " "	2,485	2.7	4	4.7
1 " "	44,436	48.8	35	41.2
2 per month	7,756	8.5	7	8.2
1 " "	625	.7	1	1.2
Movies shown during winter only				
7 per week	1,754	1.9	1	1.2
2 " "	1,562	1.7	1	1.2
1 " "	21,664	23.9	18	21.2
2 per month	1,208	1.3	2	2.4
1 " "	418	.5	1	1.2
Movies shown but frequency not known	6,256	6.9	10	11.8
Total number where motion pictures are shown	90,931	100.	85	100.
Total number where motion pictures are not shown	23,317[2]		24	
Totals	114,248		109	

[2] Of this number new chapels now being completed will make it possible for 6,952 to see movies in two prisons.

Eight per cent indicated they would not show movies even if they could, while 8 per cent did not answer the question.

It is to be noted that in institutions with 55 per cent of the convict population upon the basis of the sample of 90,931, motion pictures are shown one or more times a week during the entire year; and in institutions with about 28 per cent of the population, motion pictures are shown one or more times a week during the winter months only. Attendance is not always compulsory and the total prison population does not always get to see the same picture in a body. The inmates are frequently divided into groups among whom the privilege of motion-picture attendance is rotated. It seems that a large proportion of the prison population has the opportunity to witness motion pictures about as frequently as the normal population.

A. Selection of Pictures

Motion pictures are selected largely, as is indicated in Table 2, by the superintendent of the institution or a mem-

TABLE 2
AGENT SELECTING PICTURES

	Number	Per Cent
Superintendent or deputies	37	39
Member of school staff	17	18
Theater or distributor	13	14
Film board of trade	7	7
Chaplain	4	4
Clerk in institution	3	3
State purchasing agent	3	3
Board of welfare	2	2
Inmate	1	1
University extension	1	1
Blank	8	8
Totals	96	100

ber of his staff, this being the case in 64 per cent of a sample of 96 institutions.

The state purchasing agent selects the pictures in 3 instances, the board of welfare in 2, an inmate in 1, the university extension in 1, and in 20 cases or 21 per cent of the institutions films are selected by the distributor, by the theater, or by a film board of trade. Fifty-one, or 53 per cent, of the institutional heads indicated that some principles were followed in the selection of motion pictures shown to inmates. Nineteen, or 20 per cent, state that they follow no principles in selecting pictures, and 26, or 27 per cent, did not respond to that question. In institutions where some principles are followed in the selection of motion pictures, "gun-thrillers," "pictures in which crime is glorified," "prison and court pictures," and "sex pictures" are most frequently mentioned as types of pictures avoided; while "educational," "morally clean," "entertaining," "western," and "comic pictures" are most frequently indicated as types of pictures chosen.

In responding to the question "Do you experience any difficulty in obtaining the type of picture you want?", 19, or 20 per cent, of the institutional heads indicated that they had difficulty because "good pictures were scarce"; 25, or 26 per cent, indicated that they did because of lack of equipment or finance, institutions not having the "talkie" apparatus especially being greatly restricted in pictures to choose from; and 40, or 42 per cent, of the institutional heads stated that they had no difficulty in obtaining the type of picture they desired, while 12, or 12 per cent, did not respond to the question.

B. Quality of Pictures

From the lists of the last ten pictures shown which the heads of institutions were asked to include in their schedules,

TABLE 3

DO YOU EXPERIENCE ANY DIFFICULTY IN OBTAINING THE
TYPE OF PICTURE YOU WANT?

Answer	Number	Per Cent
Yes, "good pictures are scarce"	19	20
Yes, for reasons of equipment or finance	25	26
No	40	42
Blank	12	12
Totals	96	100

a list was compiled for the purpose of evaluating as far as possible pictures shown to inmates. This was done separately for pictures shown in penitentiaries and reformatories and those presented in correctional and training schools. A list of pictures shown during the year 1930 in a state training school for delinquent girls was also obtained and rated as a means of estimating their value. The ratings of pictures which appear in the magazine *Educational Screen* were used for evaluation of pictures shown to the inmates of correctional and penal institutions. These ratings are used widely by teachers, parents, and leaders of children and adolescents. Tables 4, 5, and 6 summarize the *Educational Screen* ratings [3] as applied to the pictures shown in the institutions.

[3] *Educational Screen* uses no system of uniform classifications in its ratings. Consequently for summary purposes five categories were devised: (1) Recommended; (2) good, interesting, entertaining; (3) mediocre, harmless; (4) questionable; (5) not advised. The ratings given for the pictures readily lent themselves to summarization under these headings: "Recommended" included such ratings as: "excellent," "notable," "very good," "worth seeing," etc. "Good, interesting, entertaining," included "entertaining," "rather charming," "interesting," "good," etc. "Mediocre, harmless," included "harmless," "perhaps funny," "of little interest," "negligible," "fair," etc. "Questionable" included "doubtful," "perhaps," "good if not too exciting," "fine if not too strong," etc. "Not advised" included "hardly," "no," "decidedly no," "too strong," "unwholesome," etc.

Table 4

SUMMARY OF RATINGS BY *EDUCATIONAL SCREEN* OF
PICTURES SHOWN IN PENITENTIARIES AND
REFORMATORIES [4]

	For Intelligent Adults		Youth (15 – 20)		Children (under 15)	
	Number	Per Cent	Number	Per Cent	Number	Per Cent
Recommended	8	15	8	15	2	4
Good, interesting, entertaining	22	41	16	30	8	15
Mediocre, harmless	11	21	9	17	5	9
Questionable	3	6	6	11	11	21
Not advised	9	17	14	27	27	51
Totals	53	100	53	100	53	100

Table 5

SUMMARY OF RATINGS BY *EDUCATIONAL SCREEN* OF
PICTURES SHOWN IN TRAINING AND
CORRECTIONAL SCHOOLS [5]

	For Intelligent Adults		Youth (15–20)		Children (under 15)	
	Number	Per Cent	Number	Per Cent	Number	Per Cent
Recommended	13	12	23	22	7	7
Good, interesting, entertaining	39	37	26	25	20	19
Mediocre, harmless	30	29	20	19	8	8
Questionable	22	21	29	27	40	38
Not advised	1	1	7	7	30	28
Totals	105	100	105	100	105	100

[4] Sample of 21 institutions.
[5] Sample of 46 institutions.

Table 6

SUMMARY OF RATINGS BY *EDUCATIONAL SCREEN* OF
PICTURES SHOWN IN A STATE TRAINING SCHOOL
FOR GIRLS

	For Intelligent Adults		Youth (15–20)		Children (under 15)	
	Number	Per Cent	Number	Per Cent	Number	Per Cent
Recommended	0	0	3	15	2	10
Good, interesting, entertaining	8	40	4	20	3	15
Mediocre, harmless	6	30	5	25	3	15
Questionable	1	5	2	10	2	10
Not advised	5	25	6	30	10	50
Totals	20	100	20	100	20	100

It is evident that of the pictures presented in penitentiaries and reformatories, to a population ranging in age from about 16 through adulthood only 15 per cent are "recommended," 41 per cent are "good, interesting, entertaining," 21 per cent are "mediocre or harmless," 6 per cent are "questionable" and 17 per cent "not advised" for "intelligent adults." Thus 56 per cent are either recommended or listed as good, interesting, or entertaining for intelligent adults, 21 per cent are mediocre or harmless, and 23 per cent are questionable or not advised. The ratings for youth from the ages of 15 to 20 are also applicable to the penitentiary and reformatory population, because a large percentage of inmates fall in this age range. For youth it will be noted, when the categories are combined, that 45 per cent are recommended or rated as good, interesting, entertaining; 17 per cent are listed as mediocre, harmless; while 38 per cent are rated questionable or not advised.

The ratings for youth (ages 15 to 20) are most applicable, for an evaluation, to the pictures presented in training and correctional schools, for the large majority of inmates in these institutions fall into this age group. Twenty-two per cent of the pictures are recommended, 25 per cent rated as good, interesting, or entertaining; 19 per cent as mediocre or harmless; 27 per cent as questionable, and 7 per cent are not advised.

Finally in the smaller sample of twenty pictures shown during the past year in a state training school for delinquent girls and young women, where the ratings for youth are also most appropriate, only 15 per cent of the pictures are recommended; 20 per cent are listed as good, interesting, entertaining, 25 per cent as mediocre or harmless, 10 per cent as questionable; and 30 per cent are not advised.

To summarize, of the 53 pictures shown in penitentiaries and reformatories, 6 per cent are regarded as questionable and 17 per cent not advised for intelligent adults; 11 per cent are rated questionable and 27 per cent not advised for youths from the ages of 15 to 20 years, an age range that constitutes a large proportion of reformatory population. Thus about one in every four pictures shown in penitentiaries and reformatories is of questionable value or harmful to intelligent adults, if we accept the ratings of *Educational Screen*, and about one in every three pictures is of questionable value or harmful to youths. Of the 105 pictures presented in correctional and training schools where the large majority of the population is included in the age range of 15 to 20 years, 27 per cent are listed as questionable and 7 per cent are not advised for youth (15 to 20). The low percentage of pictures not advised indicates that probably some fairly careful selection of pictures is made by the heads of correctional and training schools. Although only one out of every fourteen pictures is regarded by *Educational Screen* as distinctly harmful, one out of four are rated as of questionable value.

Let us turn now to a consideration of some effects of motion pictures on the inmates of correctional and penal institutions. This can be most conveniently done, perhaps, by studying in the order named the recreation, discipline, and reformation value of the movies shown.

C. Recreational Value of Motion Pictures[6]

Motion pictures shown in institutions are a significant form of recreation to the inmates. They are received by many as a contact with the "outside," a source of news, and, in some sense, as a liaison with the world left behind. They break the monotony and routine of institutional life and give the inmate something new, colorful, and exciting.

The following statistical data helps us to realize the importance of the motion pictures as a recreational medium in the institutional situation. Table 7 summarizes the responses of inmates of a state training school for girls and Table 8 of those at a large state reformatory for men, to the question "Do the movies you see here make you cheerful and contented?"

From these figures it is seen that 95 per cent of the girls and young women and 67 per cent of the boys and young men state that motion pictures presented in institutions make them cheerful and contented to some degree. Although the number of males influenced in this way is lower than the number of females, both percentages are high enough to indicate that motion pictures are regarded by the inmates as an important source of recreation.

---

[6] For our purpose an activity has "recreational value" if it diverts the individual, makes him forget his surroundings, and helps to make him cheerful and contented. He is not necessarily left in a quiescent state—on the contrary, he may be highly excited.

TABLE 7

"DO THE MOVIES YOU SEE HERE MAKE YOU CHEERFUL
AND CONTENTED?"

State Training School for Girls

	Number	Per Cent
Very much	39	16
Much	33	13
Some	130	53
Very little	31	13
Never	8	3
Blank	5	2
Totals	246	100

TABLE 8

"DO THE MOVIES YOU SEE HERE MAKE YOU CHEERFUL
AND CONTENTED?"

State Reformatory for Men

	Number	Per Cent
Very much	36	17
Much	13	6
Some	64	31
Very little	26	13
Never	37	18
Blank	31	15
Totals	207	100

The judgments of institutional heads on the recreational effect of pictures shown to inmates is essentially in accord with the above responses. When asked to indicate freely what they felt were the more important effects of motion pictures upon inmates, the 61 of the sample of 96 that replied answered as follows:

	Number	Per Cent
Made them more contented or of recreational value	45	74
Helps discipline or morale	9	15
Educational or reformation value	7	11
Totals	61	100

Thus, in 74 per cent of the cases the movies were felt by superintendents and wardens of correctional and penal institutions to be primarily recreational and effective in making inmates more cheerful and contented.

Motion-picture preferences.—On the assumption that pictures which appeal to the person have the highest recreational value [7] we may present the following information on the motion-picture preferences of inmates. Table 9 summarizes the responses of delinquent girls and young women to the request to rank a list of types of pictures in the order in which they like them best. For purposes of convenience only the first three choices are presented.

It is to be noted that "wild west" pictures are preferred by 37 per cent of the girls as a first choice; "love pictures" come next as a first choice. The combined totals of passionate love pictures and mild love pictures are 26 per cent, and mystery pictures rank third as a first choice, with 15 per cent of the girls expressing a preference for this type. When the first three choices are summated, we discover that 70 per cent of the girls indicate mild or passionate love pictures as a first, second, or third choice. Fifty-nine per cent indicate mystery pictures and 58 per cent indicate "wild west" pictures as a first, second, or third choice. Most of the girls, therefore, prefer to see love, mystery, and "wild west" pictures in the order named.

[7] This may be a questionable assumption.

Table 9

MOTION–PICTURE PREFERENCES [8]

State Training School for Girls

Type of Picture	First Rank		Second Rank		Third Rank		Sum of First Three Ranks [9]	
	No.	%	No.	%	No.	%	No.	%
Wild west pictures	90	37	32	14	16	7	138	58
Passionate love	46	19	36	15	19	8	101	42
Mystery	36	15	55	23	51	22	142	59
Airplane or adventure	17	7	21	9	31	14	69	29
Mild love	16	7	32	14	20	9	68	28
Religious	14	6	16	7	21	9	51	21
Comedies	7	3	21	9	42	18	70	29
Crime	7	3	15	6	11	5	33	14
News reels	6	2	4	2	9	4	19	8
Serials	1	1	5	2	9	4	15	6
Totals	240	100	237	100	229	100		

Of a sample of 40 inmates [10] of a large state reformatory for men, 35 who responded to this question expressed their preference for motion pictures in the following manner. Twenty-six, or 74 per cent, indicated that they preferred mystery pictures as a first, second, or third choice. Twenty-three, or 66 per cent, expressed a preference for comedies as a first, second, or third choice. Eighteen, or 51 per cent, expressed a preference for mild or passionate love pictures as a first, second, or third choice. Nine, or 26 per cent, preferred news reels as first, second, or third choice; and the same number preferred religious or sad pictures. Crime pictures and airplane or adventure pictures were preferred

[8] The types of pictures are listed for convenience in the order of their first choice preference—this is not the order in which they appear on the questionnaire.

[9] The base used for the percentages in all our ranking tables in the "Sum of the first three ranks" is the number of "first rank" responses—in this instance, 240. In the light of the crudity of the data and the procedure employed, these percentages should be regarded as very rough indexes of preferences or rankings.

[10] Our sample of male convicts at some points, due to some difficulties of access, was unavoidably restricted. The small samples are presented for what they are worth. However, we use them only when other materials we possess seem to make them fairly descriptive of the situation.

by 6, or 17 per cent, in each case as a first, second, or third choice. Among boys and young men therefore, mystery, comedies, and mild and passionate love pictures are preferred in the order named.[11]

Comparative appeal of the movies.—For purposes of getting some idea of the attractiveness of motion pictures as compared with other institutional activities, inmates were asked to rank a list presented to them, in the order in which the activities appealed to them. Tables 10 and 11 are a summary of the responses, arranged in the order of first-choice preference.

Outdoor athletics, training for a job, and band concerts are given by girls and young women in this state training

TABLE 10

COMPARATIVE APPEAL OF ACTIVITIES

State Training School for Girls

Activity	First Rank		Second Rank		Third Rank		Sum of First Three Ranks	
	No.	%	No.	%	No.	%	No.	%
Outdoor athletics	60	25	40	16	20	8	120	50
Training for a job	53	22	27	11	17	7	97	40
Band concerts	35	15	24	10	23	10	82	34
Movies	28	12	44	18	29	12	101	42
School work	20	8	41	17	44	18	105	44
Chapel service	16	7	13	5	21	9	50	21
Shop or outdoor work	9	4	12	5	12	5	33	14
Theatrical performance	7	3	9	4	16	7	32	13
Reading— library	6	3	20	8	25	11	51	21
Indoor games	3	1	6	2	4	2	13	5
Radio program	3	1	7	3	20	8	30	12
Conversation	1	0	5	2	9	2	15	6
Totals	241	100	248	100	240	100		

[11] If "recreational value" is regarded, other than as we have defined it, to include activities which lead to a state of relaxation or quiescence, it is probable that love, mystery, and wild western pictures would not be regarded as possessing recreational value. It is important, therefore, to note the use of the term.

school in preference to motion pictures as a first choice. Motion pictures, however, are preferred to school work, chapel service, shop or outdoor work, reading in the library, indoor games, radio programs, and conversation. When the first three choices are combined, we find that 50 per cent of the girls indicated outdoor athletics as a first, second, or third choice. Forty-four per cent indicated school work and 42 per cent indicated motion pictures as a first, second, or third choice in the list of twelve activities.

Among the male inmates of a large state reformatory preferences were given as follows:

TABLE 11

COMPARATIVE APPEAL OF ACTIVITIES

State Reformatory for Men

Activities	First Rank		Second Rank		Third Rank		Sum of First Three Ranks	
	No.	%	No.	%	No.	%	No.	%
Outdoor athletics	72	44	33	20	13	8	118	73
Training for a job	34	21	18	11	14	9	66	41
Shop or outdoor work	11	7	17	10	11	7	39	24
Band concerts	10	6	10	6	8	5	28	17
Movies	9	5	14	9	19	12	42	26
Reading—library	9	5	14	9	19	12	42	26
School work	5	3	17	10	14	9	36	22
Theatrical performance	4	3	10	6	7	4	21	13
Chapel service	3	2	3	2	12	8	18	12
Radio program	3	2	8	5	16	10	27	17
Indoor games	1	1	16	10	12	8	29	18
Conversation	1	1	2	1	13	8	16	10
Totals	162	100	162	100	158	100		

Outdoor athletics, training for a job, outdoor work, and band concerts appeal to male inmates more than do the motion pictures, as is evidenced by the order of the expression of first-choice preferences. The movies, on the other hand, are preferred to school work, theatrical performances, chapel services, radio programs, indoor games, and conversation. When the first three choices are combined, 73 per cent indicate a preference for outdoor athletics as a first, second, or third choice; 41 per cent indicate a similar liking for training for a job; motion pictures and the library come third, each having a percentage of 26. When the first three choices are combined, two activities—outdoor athletics and training for a job in the case of the males, and outdoor athletics and school work in the case of the females—are preferred to motion pictures; with the girls and young women indicating the higher preference for the movies than the boys and young men in the institutions. The fact that 42 per cent of the girls and 26 per cent of the men rank movies as a first, second, or third choice among a list of twelve activities indicates that motion pictures are comparatively highly regarded by inmates.

D. Discipline Value of Motion Pictures

Motion pictures may be helpful in maintaining institutional morale and discipline in two ways. Prison officials may use them as threats, prohibiting motion picture attendance for the infraction of regulations and thus putting a premium on good behavior. In addition motion pictures may work in a positive way, by instilling a cheerful and contented attitude which conduces to the observance of institution rules.

Putting premium on good behavior.—To the extent that inmates enjoy the motion pictures, the threat to deprive them of the privilege of seeing them in the event of any violation of rules may be an effective means of maintaining discipline.[12]

Seventy-one, or 74 per cent of the institutional heads from whom questionnaire material has been secured prohibit attendance for the infraction of regulations; while 25, or 26 per cent, do not. Sixty-four, or 66 per cent, of the institutional heads state that the prohibition of motion picture attendance for violation of rules helps as a disciplinary measure; 13, or 14 per cent, feel that it does not; and 19, or 20 per cent, did not answer the question.

Positive influence through cheerful, contented attitude.—The extent to which inmates are made cheerful and contented during the period of their incarceration undoubtedly is closely related to the problem of morale and discipline within the institution. A cheerful, contented outlook is as a rule conducive to the observance of institutional regulations. Table 12 summarizes the responses of institutional heads to the question "How much do you think the movies presented help in maintaining discipline?" These materials are cited at this point because when asked to "explain as fully as possible the reason for their answer" most of the wardens and superintendents made the following typical comments: "tedium and confinement relieved"; "prevents discontent—pleasurable anticipation aroused"; "lessens tendency to break regulations"; "offers relaxation and change"; "only form of entertainment." It is to be noted that 76 per cent of the institutional heads agree that movies are helpful to some degree in the maintenance of discipline.

[12] *Female, white, 17, sexual delinquent.*—Movies help you to keep out of trouble here in a way you would never suspect. There is nothing here you can do that is really bad, except running away; when we are impudent or disagreeable our punishment is to lose an entertainment. Movies and dances and once in a while a recital or something special are our only means of entertainment. Every girl enjoys a movie. Therefore, we all try to stay out of trouble so we will see the next show. A show is the most important event in ———— to most of us. It is for me at any rate.

TABLE 12
"HOW MUCH DO YOU THINK THE MOVIES PRESENTED
HELP IN MAINTAINING DISCIPLINE?"

	Number	Per Cent
Distinctly favorable	40	41
Mainly favorable	17	18
Sometimes favorable	16	17
Of no noticeable effect	9	9
Sometimes unfavorable	0	0
Mainly unfavorable	0	0
Distinctly unfavorable	0	0
Blank	14	15
Totals	96	100

Comparative value of pictures.—To estimate the value of motion pictures in comparison with other institutional activities, the wardens and superintendents were asked to rank a series of institutional activities in the order in which they were judged as helpful in maintaining discipline. Table 13 presents the results.

TABLE 13
ACTIVITIES RANKED IN ORDER OF IMPORTANCE IN
MAINTAINING DISCIPLINE

Activity	First Rank		Second Rank		Third Rank		Sum of First Three Ranks	
	No.	%	No.	%	No.	%	No.	%
Shop or outdoor work	22	30	6	10	4	6	32	43
Outdoor athletics	20	27	17	27	17	25	54	72
Schools	15	20	11	17	8	12	34	45
Chapel	10	13	12	19	6	9	28	37
Indoor games	4	5	3	5	9	13	16	21
Radio programs	2	3	2	3	2	3	6	8
Band concerts	1	1	0	0	4	6	5	7
Conversation	1	1	2	3	2	3	5	7
Movies	0	0	6	10	7	11	13	17
Theatrical performance	0	0	2	3	1	1	3	4
Reading	0	0	2	3	7	11	9	12
Totals	75	100	63	100	67	100		

We see that in no instance were motion pictures ranked first in comparison with other activities listed as factors in the maintenance of discipline. When the first three ranks of each activity are combined, we find that 72 per cent of the institutional heads ranked outdoor athletics as first, second, or third in the maintenance of discipline; 45 per cent ranked schools first, second, or third; 43 per cent ranked shop or outdoor work likewise; 37 per cent ranked chapel first, second, or third; 21 per cent indoor games; and only 17 per cent ranked the motion pictures as first, second, or third as a factor in the maintenance of discipline. Motion pictures, however, are regarded as more important in this respect than radio programs, band concerts, theatrical performances, reading, or conversation. It seems, therefore, that although motion pictures play some part in the maintenance of institutional discipline they are relatively unimportant in this respect as compared to other activities.

Love pictures and discipline.—Not all pictures which appeal to inmates and please them are conducive to the observance of institutional regulations. As has been indicated earlier in this chapter, mild or passionate love pictures appeal strongly to male and female inmates, 70 per cent of the girls and young women and 51 per cent of the boys and young men ranking these as first, second, or third in order of preference. In the institutional situation, where not only are the sexes segregated and thus natural sex problems created but where also many of the inmates are sexual delinquents with fixed sex habits broken by their incarceration, love pictures may give rise to serious disciplinary problems.

Not only passionate love pictures but also mild ones, or even the appearance of one of the opposite sex on the screen, may in the institutional situation arouse the passion of observers. The stirring of sex impulses is discernible in both male and female institutions. To give a picture of the personal experiences of the inmates who are so affected, we are presenting a few typical accounts:

Female, white, 17, sexual delinquent.—After I have seen a very thrilling love picture here I always feel very passionate. I feel like I want someone to take me and love me. . . . When I see a passionate love picture here it just stirs me up so. I like to see them very much. *Very often* I long for someone to love me passionately. I don't know why I should feel that way, but I do.

Female, white, 18, sexual delinquent.—Another picture which caused some of the matrons to get flustered over was ———— in ————. Gee, but that picture had an effect, and how! I would have given anything to have been with my boy friend again. O yes, the picture had that effect on many of the girls, I know.

Female, white, 16, sexual delinquent.—They make me think of the times I used to have and wish that I could be loved by some man too, if it is a passionate love picture or just a love picture. They make me remember what I was doing when I was out, and of the times I used to make whoopee. They make me think lots, when they are making love; whether it is real or just put on. And it makes me think if I could only be the one instead of looking at it.

Male, white, 18, sentenced for burglary, inmate of reformatory.—Now, love pictures are the movies I care for; at least I get a kick out of them. I should say I do love to see them, and how! They make me feel as though I could love the death out of a girl. See my girl, and then I suppose you will know the rest without my telling you.

Male, white, 23, sentenced for rape, ex-convict.—"Sure I got excited when I saw a passionate picture. I used to get the blues over some of them love pictures and I often got torrid over a couple of 'fraus' who were on the screen."

The extent to which motion pictures stir inmates sexually is suggested in Tables 14, 15, and 16.

Table 14
"DO MOVIES SHOWN HERE STIR YOU SEXUALLY?"
State Training School for Girls

	Number	Per Cent
Very much	31	13
Much	31	13
Some	49	20
Very little	71	29
Never	60	24
Blank	4	1
Totals	246	100

Table 15
"DO THE MOVIES SHOWN HERE STIR YOU SEXUALLY?"
State Reformatory for Boys and Young Men

	Number	Per Cent
Very much	2	5
Much	2	5
Some	15	38
Very little	8	20
Never	10	25
Blank	3	8
Totals	40	100

Table 16
"DID THE MOVIES IN THE INSTITUTION STIR YOU SEXUALLY?"
Ex-Convicts

	Number	Per Cent
Very much	4	6
Much	2	3
Some	12	17
Very little	18	25
Never	33	46
Blank	2	3
Totals	71	100

In terms of these tables it is seen that about 75 per cent of the girls and young women admit being sexually aroused to some degree by the presentation of motion pictures. About 68 per cent of the male delinquents and criminals and about 51 per cent of the ex-convicts admit a similar influence.

Becoming sexually aroused does not necessarily create disciplinary problems. Some inmates grow disconsolate or melancholy, a condition which may result in sullenness but which does not necessarily result in misconduct. Other inmates may curb their sex desires, or divert their mind to other things.

Male, Negro, 22, sentenced for burglary, inmate of reformatory.—When I see a love picture it gives me a somewhat passionate feeling. I like to see love pictures once in a while. They stir me up a little sometimes. When I would see love pictures sometimes, my cell partners and I would sit in the cell and tell each other about our experiences with girls that we have come in contact with. I would wish that it would not be long before I could be out with one of my old girls. Sometimes when I would see a love picture it would make me lonesome and blue. I would long to be with one of my girl friends. And sometimes when they would have a love picture I would not go to the show to keep from having that old downhearted feeling that makes me sometimes want to cry to satisfy my feelings.

Male, white, 28, sentenced for robbery, ex-convict.—Love scenes used to make me think of outside and women I had been with. Sometimes it aroused my passions and I'd have a few hours of unbearable desire but I would think of other things and let my passion exhaust itself and wear away.

Male, white, 23, sentenced for robbery, inmate of reformatory.—When I see passionate love pictures here, I feel that I would like to be free and have some girl to love. Yes, I like to see them. Yes, at times they stir me up. There is nothing to do after you see them but to think about them. I have not had enough experience to describe; the name of the picture I do not know, but I felt that I would like to be free and do the same thing. I did nothing but went to my cell and read all of the love stories that I could find.

The arousing of sex passion by the movies may, however, lead to autoerotic and homosexual practices. Masturbation and homosexuality may be practiced by inmates of either sex.[1]

The pictures may therefore on the one hand be a source of great pleasure to inmates and on the other hand give rise to some problems of discipline. They are not to be thought of in any sense as the cause of the problems of sex in penal or correctional institutions. Such problems prevailed before the introduction of motion pictures. Nevertheless, motion pictures may serve as an agency inciting some to sex passion and so contributing to what is regarded in institutions as sex misconduct.

E. REFORMATION VALUE OF MOTION PICTURES

Motion pictures in a number of ways play some part in instilling the desire to reform. Before scenes of home life or of attractive and carefree behavior shown in the movies, institutional life becomes even more undesirable and burdensome by comparison. In many cases this contrast makes inmates realize more vividly the futility and price of delinquent or criminal activity, and they determine to abandon their old ways of living. Many pictures bring up images of the past in the minds of inmates and in reflecting about and reëvaluating their experiences the desire to abandon a delinquent or criminal career frequently emerges. Some pictures stressing the moral, "Crime does not pay," and portraying punishment make an especially deep impression in the institutional situation. Finally, pictures showing the

[1] Autobiographical material on this point has been omitted.

achievement of success through struggle and the overcoming of many obstacles may instill both the desire to succeed on a conventional level and courage to make the attempt. These influences are quite clear in the following autobiographical accounts.

Male, white, 23, sentenced for robbery, inmate of reformatory.— Some of the movies that you see here make you think about home and the things that you did that you ought not to have done. Yes, they make me think very much. The most important thought that they make me think about is home with my mother and brother. The kind of movies that make me think most is a picture in which some poor girl or boy has got into trouble. Most of the movies that you see here teach you to behave yourself when you get out and to go straight. Yes, they teach you very much if you will take notice of them. The most important things that you learn from them is to never steal and not to run around with bad company. The kind of movies that teach you most is a sad picture or where some boy or girl gets into trouble and causes the mother a lot of worry. . . . The feeling that I have when I see crime pictures makes me think of the things that I did and want another chance to make good. I do not think that such movies are true to life. I don't know that they give me new ideas on how to pull a job and fool the police. Yes, the punishment given to criminals in such movies makes me want to go straight and to keep out of trouble.

Male, Negro, 24, sentenced for robbery, inmate of reformatory.— Some of the movies make me think of the outside and the times I've had when I was out in the free world—also of the great mistake I've made in life. And if I had the chance to make good how I could try hard to stay out of this and all the rest of the institutions. The most important thing is how to stay on the outside and make a man of myself when I'm out there again. And I also have learned what kind of company to keep on the outside.

Female, white, 17, sexual delinquent.—When I see a picture of women that go wrong, such as "The Primrose Path," I see where I have erred in my own way of living and how I could have missed all that, if I would have just used my head. Some of these kinds of pictures are really in good form, and I think true to life. I like to see a picture like that, but I cannot truthfully say that I should like to copy their examples. The endings of these pictures show you what such actions and deeds come to, so you want to avoid it. In a way it makes you stay out of trouble. I have done wrong and am now taking punishment. I have seen what happens in a show but I was too dumb to take the hint. Now, though, I think I shall never lower myself again.

Male, white, 20, sentenced for robbery, inmate of penal institution.—By looking ahead to my future they help me to go straight. Pictures of the country or city mostly do this. Yes, there are other things here that help you to go straight. They are the schools where you learn a good trade which you can follow after you get out.

Male, Negro, 22, sentenced for burglary, inmate of reformatory.—The most important things that I think about are as follows: going straight, getting a job so I can look the world in the face and say, I worked for my car and my clothes. The kinds of pictures that make me think are the kinds that show how a man works from the bottom and at the end is prosperous, by working honestly. When he had many difficulties to overcome he never gave up, but kept on striving hard until he won at the end. The movies that I see here teach me how to get the best out of life honestly. . . . When I see movies that show people with good automobiles, money and good clothes, it makes me feel as if I have been cut out for bad luck. When I see movies of that type it makes me feel ashamed of my cheap clothes and the way I live. I have often wished that I had a good car, good clothes, plenty of money, and a swell home to live in. That is part of the reason for my criminal career because when I would see a picture like that it would encourage me to go and try to break into someone's property.

These kind of pictures now make me think most of the time when I can make honest money. I have come to the conclusion when I get out to work until I have made enough money to open myself up a shoe shining parlor. I wish that I could live the last six years of my life over again.

We do not see crime pictures down here because they are forbidden to be shown in this institution. If they were allowed to show them, I don't think I would be interested in seeing them now. The pictures that I have seen here have helped me in lots of ways to go straight. The pictures help me go straight by teaching me how to make money honestly. How to live and how to be decent and respectable to people that I am forced to come into contact with, when I am free on the streets again.

Female, white, 17, sexual delinquent.—Most of the movies here make me think of home and the good times I had outside. The movies here make me think a good deal. The more important things I think about are what I want to do when I get out of here. Love pictures usually make me think the most. *Some* of the movies here have made me see some of the mistakes I've made. I learn quite a lot from the movies. The more important things I have learned from the movies is how I can be good and yet have a good time. Pictures that show the home life and love pictures teach me the most. . . . Some of the movies here make me think of getting married and settling down, but not very many make me feel that way. Pictures that show where a young couple have gotten married and are happy and soon children come, make me feel that way. I get ideas from the movies of what kind of a husband I would like to have. I want a husband that will always love me and be good to me, someone that can support me and make me happy. I have *never* had the feeling that I would like to marry for money.

The following statistical data give us some idea of the extent to which motion pictures influence the reformation of offenders. Tables 17 and 18 summarize the responses of inmates to the question "Do the movies make you feel like keeping out of trouble or make you feel like going straight?"

It is to be noted that 84 per cent of the girls and young women and 61 per cent of the boys and young men indicated that motion pictures shown in institutions make them feel

TABLE 17

"DO THE MOVIES MAKE YOU FEEL LIKE GOING STRAIGHT?"

State Reformatory For Men

	Number	Per Cent
Very much	68	33
Much	15	7
Some	36	17
Very little	8	4
Never	33	16
Blank	47	23
Totals	207	100

TABLE 18

"DO THE MOVIES MAKE YOU FEEL LIKE KEEPING OUT OF TROUBLE?"

State Training School for Girls and Young Women

	Number	Per Cent
Very much	55	22
Much	33	13
Some	84	34
Very little	37	15
Never	36	15
Blank	1	1
Totals	246	100

in some degree like keeping out of trouble or going straight. This quite obviously does not tell us in any way of the number of inmates who actually reform, but it does suggest that motion pictures may be a factor in reformation.

Yet, the significance of motion pictures as an agency of reformation seems slight in the eyes of inmates, when compared with other activities of institutional life. This can be seen in Tables 19 and 20.

TABLE 19

RANKING OF ACTIVITIES IN ORDER OF THEIR IMPOR-
TANCE AS FACTORS IN REFORMATION

State Reformatory for Men

Activity	First Rank		Second Rank		Third Rank		Sum of First Three Ranks	
	No.	%	No.	%	No.	%	No.	%
Training for a job	52	38	24	18	9	7	85	62
Shop or outdoor work	22	16	20	15	11	9	53	39
Outdoor athletics	18	13	29	21	23	18	70	51
Chapel service	14	10	8	6	16	12	38	28
School work	9	7	9	7	9	7	27	20
Band concerts	6	4	4	3	4	3	14	10
Reading	6	4	15	11	26	20	47	34
Conversation	4	3	6	4	4	3	14	10
Movies	2	2	7	5	10	8	19	14
Theatrical performance	2	2	1	1	3	2	6	4
Indoor games	2	2	6	4	8	6	16	12
Radio program	0	0	7	5	6	5	13	9
Totals	137	100	136	100	129	100		

TABLE 20

RANKING OF ACTIVITIES IN ORDER OF THEIR IMPORTANCE
AS FACTORS IN KEEPING GIRLS OUT OF TROUBLE

State Training School For Girls and Young Women

Activity	First Rank		Second Rank		Third Rank		Sum of First Three Ranks	
	No.	%	No.	%	No.	%	No.	%
Training for job	122	50	33	14	19	9	174	72
School work	49	20	53	23	38	17	140	58
Chapel service	20	8	33	14	37	17	90	37
Outdoor athletics	19	8	36	16	22	10	77	32
Band concerts	10	4	7	3	9	4	26	11
Movies	7	3	8	4	12	6	27	11
Shop or outdoor work	6	3	13	6	17	8	36	15
Reading—library	5	2	25	11	47	21	77	32
Conversation	2	1	11	5	12	6	25	10
Theatrical performance	2	1	7	3	3	1	12	5
Indoor games	0	0	5	2	4	2	9	4
Totals	242	100	231	100	220	100		

It is to be noted that only 2 per cent of the males in the state reformatory ranked motion pictures first in the list of activities presented, while 38 per cent of them ranked training for a job first, 16 per cent shop or outdoor work, 13 per cent outdoor athletics, 10 per cent chapel service, 7 per cent school work, 4 per cent band concerts and reading, and 3 per cent conversation. Among the girls and young women only 3 per cent ranked motion pictures first in the list of factors presented as most important in keeping them out of trouble after their release; while 50 per cent ranked training for a job first, 20 per cent school work, 8 per cent chapel service, 8 per cent outdoor athletics, and 4 per cent band concerts.

When the first three ranks are combined among the boys and young men we find that 62 per cent of the population ranked training for a job first, second, or third in its estimated importance in helping them to go straight after their release; 51 per cent ranked outdoor athletics as first, second, or third in its importance in this respect; 39 per cent shop or outdoor work; 34 per cent reading, 28 per cent chapel service, 20 per cent school work, and only 14 per cent ranked motion pictures as first, second, or third in its importance as a factor in reformation.

Among the girls and young women 72 per cent ranked training for a job first, second, or third in its estimated importance in keeping them out of trouble after their release; 58 per cent ranked school work as first, second, or third in this respect; 37 per cent chapel service, 32 per cent outdoor athletics; 32 per cent reading; 15 per cent shop and outdoor work; while 11 per cent ranked motion pictures first, second, or third in its importance as a factor in reformation.

It is evident, therefore, that it is the opinion of inmates that although the motion pictures play some part in their reformation they are relatively unimportant compared to other institutional activities.

It is interesting to note the opinions of heads of correctional and penal institutions on the reformation value of motion pictures. Table 21 summarizes their responses to the question "How much do you think the movies shown help the prisoner to go straight after his release?"

Table 21

REFORMATION VALUE OF MOTION PICTURES IN THE OPINION OF HEADS OF CORRECTIONAL AND PENAL INSTITUTIONS

	Number	Per Cent
Distinctly favorable	5	5
Mainly favorable	4	4
Sometimes favorable	19	20
No noticeable effect	36	38
Sometimes unfavorable	2	2
Mainly unfavorable	0	0
Distinctly unfavorable	0	0
Blank	30	31
Totals	96	100

Twenty-nine per cent of the institutional heads feel that the motion pictures are to some degree favorable to reformation.

When asked to indicate the comparative value of motion pictures as a factor in reformation, the heads of correctional and penal institutions were, on the whole, in striking agreement with the inmates.

It is to be noted that in no case did an institutional head rank the movies first in importance among the activities listed, in the reformation of offenders. When the first three rankings of the 96 institutional heads who ranked the activi-

TABLE 22

RANK OF ACTIVITIES AS FACTORS IN INDIVIDUAL
REFORMATION

In the Opinion of Heads of Correctional and Penal Institutions

Activity	First Rank		Second Rank		Third Rank		Sum of First Three Ranks	
	No.	%	No.	%	No.	%	No.	%
Shop or outdoor work	21	26	7	10	6	9	34	43
Chapel services	20	25	12	16	6	9	38	48
Vocational training	18	23	16	22	6	9	40	51
Schools	14	18	15	21	20	30	49	62
Outdoor athletics	6	8	9	13	7	11	22	28
Reading	0	0	8	11	14	21	22	28
Movies	0	0	1	1	3	5	4	5
Indoor games	0	0	2	3	1	2	3	4
Radio	0	0	2	3	1	2	3	4
Theatrical performance	0	0	0	0	0	0	0	0
Band concerts	0	0	0	0	1	2	1	1
Totals	79	100	72	100	65	100		

ties are combined, 62 per cent ranked school work as first,
second, or third in importance in the reformation of offenders; 51 per cent, vocational training; 48 per cent chapel services; 43 per cent, shop or outdoor work; 28 per cent, outdoor
athletics and reading, respectively; and only 5 per cent
ranked motion pictures as first, second, or third in importance in reforming offenders. One can see, then, that in the
judgment of heads, as well as of inmates of penal and correctional institutions, motion pictures are relatively unimportant as an agency of reformation.

It is interesting to note the responses of the institutional
heads to the question "Do you know of prisoners who have
been led by the pictures shown in the institutions to give up
lives of crime?"

	Number	Per Cent
Yes	1	1
No	74	77
Blank	21	22
Total	96	100

In only one instance was there any report of a prisoner giving up a life of crime because of the influence of motion pictures; and in this case the motion picture's influence was rather indirect because (as the warden explained) the individual secured a job with a film company.

Feelings of bitterness.—Finally, motion pictures shown to inmates may arouse feelings of bitterness and the belief that they are not receiving a "square deal." This reaction is hardly conducive to reformation, and in fact may manifest itself in a desire for revenge. Many inmates leave the correctional or penal institution with the firm desire to wreak vengeance on society for the injustice they feel has been committed in their case. This feeling may in part result from at least two types of motion pictures.

First, pictures that show forms of conduct which are usually regarded as unconventional, delinquent, or criminal, but which do not carry these qualities in the context of the picture. Pictures of this type may embitter inmates, arouse feelings of resentment against the community and make them feel they have not been justly dealt with, for, as they point out, people on the screen "get away with it," as do also other people of their own acquaintance.

Female, white, 17, sexual delinquent.—Lots of the pictures I see here make me feel that I have not had a square deal because I know a lot of girls that have got away with a lot more than I did. When I see pictures that show where a girl gets away with a lot, it makes me feel bitter.

Female, white, 16, sexual delinquent.—When I see movies like——————where young boys and girls are kissing, lying down on sofas, telling each other how much they really love, I don't think then that I am getting a fair deal. I know young girls on the outside who are doing just as we have done, go out with young boys, go with everyone that comes along. We call it puppy love. That is right.

Male, white, 23, sentenced for burglary, inmate of reformatory.— Yes, some pictures that you see here make you feel bitter toward society, and then again they make you feel that you have not had a square deal. They make me feel that way when I see the way some things are done and the things that people do and are not punished for. The kind of picture that does this is society pictures and love pictures.

The second type of picture that arouses feelings of resentment and bitterness is that which portrays wealth, society life, comfort, luxury. We have already noted how pictures may suggest the futility of delinquent or criminal behavior by presenting forms of life that contrast to that in the institutional situation; but patterns of life too sharply in contrast with the relatively bare and meager life of the institution may augment the feeling that one is not receiving justice.

Male, white, 28, sentenced for robbery, ex-convict.—I resent plays where there is too much gayety and laughter on the part of the rich—they should share in sufferings too.

Male, white, 18, sentenced for burglary, inmate of reformatory.— Well, pictures in a way make me resent society. Why? Because I'm not out there while they are. I never did have or get a square deal as yet. Because I hate them, hate them. None other but the society pictures. I just don't like them, that's all. I despise them, ignore them all.

Male, white, 27, sentenced for robbery, ex-convict.—Scenes of country roads, concrete highways, massive and beautiful public buildings, parks, etc., burn me up. People, I mean poor people, work like hell, and are taxed to pay for these things. Who gets the most out of them? The rich people do. A poor man can't pay the price that they hold to for lots or buildings on a concrete road. The rich can and still they pay the same

. amount of tax as the poor. Does a poor man ever sleep in the Executive mansion or the White House? Who pays for all these things? Who paid for the menagerie on Govenor ——'s property? The unthinking public. . . . I hate pictures of greatness and riches because in back of it all some poor guys are paying for it. I certainly do hold it against Society—isn't society and Wall Street in back of the present-day suffering and starvation? Are they starving?

In Tables 23 and 24 we see that 39 per cent of the girls and young women and 37 per cent of the boys and young men are embittered towards society to some degree by movies seen in institutions.

TABLE 23

DO MOVIES EVER MAKE YOU BITTER TOWARDS SOCIETY?
State Training School for Girls

	Number	Per Cent
Very much	15	6
Much	9	4
Some	43	17
Very little	31	12
Never	144	59
Blank	4	2
Totals	246	100

TABLE 24

DO MOVIES EVER MAKE YOU BITTER TOWARDS SOCIETY?
State Reformatory for Men

	Number	Per Cent
Very much	30	14
Much	4	2
Some	26	13
Very little	16	8
Never	88	42
Blank	43	21
Totals	207	100

F. Summary

The material in this chapter indicates that movies shown in institutions may have appreciable recreational, disciplinary, and reformatory value. Ninety-five per cent of the sample of delinquent girls in the girls' institution and 67 per cent of the boys and young men in the reformatory declare that pictures have to some extent made them feel more cheerful and contented. About 66 per cent of the institution heads feel motion pictures are helpful in maintaining discipline. Eighty-four per cent of the female delinquents and 61 per cent of the male convicts indicate that motion pictures make them feel to some extent like keeping out of trouble or going straight; and 29 per cent of the institutional heads regard movies as favorable to some degree to reformation. Nevertheless, motion pictures seem comparatively unimportant as a factor in reformation. Only 14 per cent of the male inmates, 15 per cent of the female, and 5 per cent of the institutional heads ranked motion pictures first, second, or third in order of their importance in reformation among a list of twelve activities.

Another picture is presented to us by the questionnaire responses. Motion pictures may contribute to disciplinary problems and to some extent they may embitter inmates rather than exert a reformative influence. About 75 per cent of the girls and young women, 68 per cent of the boys and young men, and 51 per cent of the ex-convicts admit being sexually aroused by motion pictures presented in the institutional situation which, in so far as it tends to auto-erotic and homosexual behavior, augments problems of sex conduct within the institutions. Certain types of pictures, it has been found, may embitter inmates and make them feel they have not been justly dealt with.

From the discussion it is reasonably clear that motion pictures shown to inmates of correctional or penal institutions may help to redirect the behavior of offenders along socially acceptable lines; yet they may also exercise the opposite influence. In the light of our earlier discussion this seeming contradiction is not strange. Motion pictures present a wide range of themes and forms of life which, added to the differences in personal inclination, may influence people to diverse and conflicting lines of conduct.

CHAPTER X
SUMMARY

A. REMARKS ON METHOD

ALTHOUGH for purposes of investigation reliance on accounts of personal experience is, in general, a controversial matter, it seems quite clear that the objection is not of great import as regards this investigation. In the light of the precautions taken in the collection of the materials—gaining the confidence of contributors, stressing the impartial character of the study, calling for concrete experiences in which the movies were involved—it seems that no serious charge can be made against the general reliability of the documents secured. This conclusion, furthermore, is attested to by the fact that although the materials were collected separately from the various contributors, similar patterns of behavior in which the motion pictures play a part can be discerned in many of them.

Our sample of autobiographical and interview materials was unavoidably less extensive than originally intended.[1] Our findings therefore, should be interpreted in terms of the samples secured. In the writers' judgment, while additional autobiographical and interview materials would be valuable they would not alter the fundamental relations of motion pictures to behavior, discovered in this study. They would undoubtedly, however, fill in and present a more clear-cut picture of the patterns traced.

[1] Ninety motion-picture life-history documents from boys in a high-rate delinquency area, 40 from male inmates of a state reformatory, 20 from female inmates of a truant and behavior-problem school, and 55 from ex-convicts were obtained. These, together with 42 stenographic interviews with delinquent boys and 18 with delinquent girls; 258 brief essays from male convicts and 118 from female inmates comprised all our personal account material. Some of these were too incomplete to be of much value.

B. SUMMARY OF FINDINGS

Rôle of motion pictures in the lives of delinquents and criminals.—It seems clear that the motion pictures were a factor of importance in the delinquent or criminal careers of about 10 per cent of the male and 25 per cent of the female offenders studied. These percentages are essentially conservative and represent the instances in which the contributors have been able to trace with confidence the influence of the movies in their own delinquent or criminal careers. In addition to these readily traced influences, motion pictures, by reason of subtle and often unconscious effects, may unwittingly dispose or lead individuals to various forms of misconduct. At least two considerations justify this conclusion: first, the number of delinquents and criminals who admit having experienced motion-picture influences of a character obviously associated with crime far exceeds the number who detect a relationship between such influences and their own criminal behavior; second, there are always some offenders who can detect in their own experience such a relation. It is reasonable to assume that what presents itself to some as a conscious factor in delinquency may operate as an unconscious factor in the experience of others.

Several important indirect influences disposing or leading persons to delinquency or crime are discernible in the experience of male offenders. Through the display of crime techniques and criminal patterns of behavior; by arousing desires for easy money and luxury, and by suggesting questionable methods for their achievement; by inducing a spirit of bravado, toughness, and adventurousness; by arousing intense sexual desires; and by invoking daydreaming of criminal rôles, motion pictures may create attitudes and furnish techniques conducive, quite unwittingly, to delinquent or criminal behavior.

One may detect in the case of delinquent girls and young women influences similar to those spoken of in the case of young men. Motion pictures may play a major or minor rôle in female delinquency and crime by arousing sexual passion, by instilling the desire to live a gay, wild, fast life, by evoking longings for luxury and smart appearance, and by suggesting to some girls questionable methods of easily attaining them; by the display of modes of beautification and love techniques; by the depiction of various forms of crime readily imitated by girls and young women; and by competing with home and school for an important place in the life of the girls.

On the other hand, movies may redirect the behavior of delinquents and criminals along socially acceptable lines and make them hesitant about, and sometimes deter them from, the commission of offenses. Through instilling the impulse to "be good," in depicting the unattractive and dangerous aspects of criminal careers, and by vividly portraying the punishment and ill fate of the violators of the moral and legal code, motion pictures may produce attitudes and furnish insights which, consciously or unwittingly, may offer some check to a delinquent or criminal career.

Yet, pictures meant to be deterrent do not always have such a desired effect. There are a number of nullifying and immunizing factors which may effectively counteract the elements in the picture meant to guide behavior along conventional paths. Among these are: the short life of the deterrent effect; yielding to temptation or group pressure; getting accustomed to the punishment shown; the lack of a sufficiently vivid portrayal of punishment; the discounting of the pictures showing the punishment of offenders; the feeling by observers that they can outwit the law; the feeling of sympathy for the criminals; or the feeling of resentment to their punishment. By reason of these attitudes and conditions the delinquent or criminal observer may not be affected by the deterrent lesson, presumably to be conveyed by a given picture. Because of the frequent inclusion in such pictures of entrancing scenes, such as those of a life of gayety, wild life, luxury, adventure, easy money, etc., the deterrent aspect may be overshadowed. The discrimination of the observer may be confused, and his subsequent difficulty in keeping apart the different "motifs" may end in a failure to get the deterrent import of the picture.

Motion pictures presented in correctional and penal institutions.—The materials we have collected reveal that motion pictures shown in penal institutions may be of recreational, disciplinary, or reformatory value. It is evident that pictures appeal to inmates, entertain and cheer them, and thus in this sense are not only recreational but are also at the same time conducive to the observance of regulations. In addition movies indirectly help in the maintenance of discipline, in so far as prohibition of attendance for the infraction of regulations places a premium on good behavior. Many pictures shown to inmates are valuable in helping, to some extent, to redirect the behavior of offenders along socially acceptable lines. In observing scenes that bring up images of the past—home life, interesting, and colorful experiences—institutional life may become even more undesirable and burdensome by comparison, and inmates may be helped to realize the futility and price of a delinquent or criminal career. Pictures with the "crime does not pay" motif may make some impression on the inmates.

On the whole, however, motion pictures have relatively little reformation value. Both inmates and institutional heads rank motion pictures as markedly inferior in reformatory value to such activities as training for a job, shop or outdoor work, outdoor athletics, chapel service, and school work. Furthermore, motion pictures may exert an influence on inmates contrary to that of discipline or reformation. Some inmates become "blue" and disconsolate after witnessing more pleasant forms of life on the screen; others grow resentful, become sullen and morose and harbor thoughts of revenge on society for the injustice they feel has been meted out to them. Such effects are not only not conducive to the observance of institutional regulations but may actually lead to disciplinary problems. Furthermore, love or sex pictures, which have great appeal to both male and female inmates, may create some problems of discipline in so far as they may lead to autoerotic or homosexual behavior.

C. Concluding Remarks

It is evident that motion pictures may exert influences in diametrically opposite directions. The movies may help to dispose or lead persons to delinquency and crime or they may fortify conventional behavior. Movies shown to inmates may cheer them and help make them contented or may make them blue and disconsolate; they may be of value in the maintenance of institutional discipline or they may create or augment problems of institutional misconduct; they may encourage reformation of the offender or they may make the inmate bitter and resentful against society. Motion pictures may create attitudes favorable to crime and the criminal or unfavorable to them.

How are these conflicting influences to be explained? As we have indicated, two conditions determine the nature and direction of the effects of motion pictures on the behavior of a given person: first, the diversity and wide range of themes depicted on the screen; and second, the social milieu, the attitudes and interests of the observer. On the one hand the social background of the person tends to be quite unconsciously the basis for the selection and interpretation of motion picture themes and patterns of behavior that in their immediate or cumulative effect may leave their imprint on him. The child in the high-rate delinquency area tends to be sensitized and the child in the low-rate delinquency area immunized to delinquent and criminal attitudes and forms of behavior depicted on the screen. On the other hand the forms of thought and behavior presented by the movies are such as to provide material and incentive to those sensitized to delinquent and criminal suggestion.

Motion pictures play an especially important part in the lives of children reared in socially disorganized areas. The influence of motion pictures seems to be proportionate to the weakness of the family, school, church, and neighborhood. Where the institutions which traditionally have transmitted social attitudes and forms of conduct have broken down, as is usually the case in high-rate delinquency areas, motion pictures assume a greater importance as a source of ideas and schemes of life.

Motion pictures are a relatively new factor in modern life. While primarily a form of recreation, they play an appreciably important rôle in developing conceptions of life and transmitting patterns of conduct. They may direct the behavior of persons along socially acceptable lines or they may lead, as has been indicated, to misconduct. They may be, therefore, an agency of social value or of social harm. As the former they raise no issue, as the latter they raise problems of social control.

APPENDIX

APPENDIX A [1]

Questionnaire Submitted to Grade-School Children

Name of school.   Grade.

Boy or girl.   Age.

Nationality.   Race.   Religion.

1. How many times during a week do you usually go to the movies?

    How many times during a week would you like to go? ———

    How many times do you usually stay thru a show?

    What movie theater do you usually go to?

    How many blocks is it from your home?

2. Must you ask your parents for permission before you can go to the movies?

    Do you ever go, even though your parents don't want you to?

3. Place the number, 1, before the kind of picture you like best, the number, 2, before the kind you like next best, the number, 3, before the kind you like next, and so on.

    (   ) Cowboy pictures   (   ) News reels
    (   ) Airplane pictures   (   ) Serials or follow-up pictures
    (   ) Love pictures   (   ) Gangster pictures
    (   ) Detective pictures   (   ) Comedies
    (   ) Spooky pictures

4. I usually go to the movies   (use check mark to show which)

         by myself   with my parents
         with brothers or sisters   with other grown-up people
         with a bunch of boys   with a boy friend
         with a bunch of girls   with a girl friend

[1] To conserve space only the printed material appearing in the forms is included. The spacing, blanks, and other questionnaire details are omitted.

5. After I see a movie I usually (use check mark to show which)
   start to play at what I have seen in the movie
   talk to my friends about the picture
   imagine myself acting like they did in the movie
   talk to my parents about the picture
   (If you usually do something else after you see a movie, tell what it is.)

6. Who are your three favorite men movie stars, and who are your three favorite women movie stars?

Men stars	*Women stars*
1.	1.
2.	2.
3.	3.

7. Place the number, 1, before the kind of movie scene you like best, the number, 2, before the kind of movie scene you like next best, the number, 3, before the kind you like next, and so on.

   ( ) Sad scenes   ( ) Religious scenes
   ( ) Spooky scenes   ( ) Fighting
   ( ) Murder scenes   ( ) Funny scenes
   ( ) Love scenes   ( ) Gun play
   ( ) Scenes which show   ( ) Scenes of unselfish
          loyalty or true   actions
          friendship.

8. Do your parents ever tell you that some movies are bad for boys and girls?
   What kind do they say are bad?
   Do you agree with them?

9. Which of the following kinds of life do the movies usually show in an interesting way? (Show by a check mark)
   College life   Honest life
   Home life   Hard work
   Life of the criminal   Fighting
   Wealthy or rich life   Having a good time.

10. Do you always want the good man in the pictures to win?
    Do you ever want the bad or tough man to win?

11. Do you and your friends talk about what you see in the movies? How much do you talk about what you see in the movies?
    a lot   once in a while
    sometimes   never

12. Do you daydream about what you see in the movies?
    How much do you this?
        a lot
        sometimes
        once in a while
        never

13. Do you and your companions play at what you see in the
    movies?   How much do you do this?
        a lot
        sometimes
        once in a while
        never

14. Would you rather be one of the good people or one of the
    bad people in these games?

15. Show by an X which of the following are good men, and by an
    0 which are bad men.
    ( ) Indians   ( ) Al Capone   ( ) Detectives
    ( ) Cowboys   ( ) George Bancroft ( ) A rich banker
    ( ) Policemen   ( ) Lon Chaney   ( ) A tough gang leader
    ( ) Robbers   ( ) Tom Mix   ( ) A wealthy bootlegger
    ( ) Soldiers   ( ) Hack Wilson   ( ) A bold bandit

16. Show by a check mark which of the following you would like
    to be. If you are a girl, indicate which you would like to have
    as your friends.
    ( ) Indians   ( ) Al Capone   ( ) Detectives
    ( ) Cowboys   ( ) George Bancroft ( ) A rich banker
    ( ) Policemen   ( ) Lon Chaney   ( ) A tough gang leader
    ( ) Robbers   ( ) Tom Mix   ( ) A wealthy bootlegger
    ( ) Soldiers   ( ) Hack Wilson   ( ) A bold bandit

17. Do any kind of motion pictures make you want to get a lot
    of money easily?
    What kind of pictures, if any, do this?

18. When you see an exciting movie do you want to (show by
    check mark)
        do something brave and daring?
        act tough or fight someone?
        go out and have a good time?
        talk to others about what you have just seen?
        start to play an exciting game?
        imagine yourself having a lot of adventure?

19. When you see a thrilling gangster, burglar, or bandit picture do you

> feel sorry for the gangster or burglar?
> feel like you want to be a gangster or burglar?
> imagine yourself being one, doing big and daring things, and fooling the police?
> want to be a policeman?
> feel that every gangster and burglar ought to be caught and punished?
> think nothing about what you have just seen?

20. Have the movies ever made you

> want to stay away from school?
> want to run away from home?
> want to go out and have a lot of fun?
> want to break into a house and take something?
> want to take things from other people?

21. Have the movies ever led you to do anything wrong, or that you feel that you shouldn't have done?
If so, what kind of picture did you see, and what did you do?

22. Have you seen any pictures which made you want to be real good?   What was the name of the picture and what was it about?
For how long were you good?

23. Do you think that the movies make boys or girls do bad things?   What, for instance?
Do you think that the movies make boys or girls do good things?   What, for instance?
Do you think that the movies make no difference on how boys or girls behave?

24. Do you think that the punishment which the bad man gets in the movies stops boys from doing bad things?

25. What kind of pictures, if any, do you think are not true to life?
Why?

26. Place the number, 1, before the one you do most, the number, 2, before the one you do next most, the number, 3, before the one you do next, and so on.

> (   ) Reading stories
> (   ) Playing or talking about what you see in the movies

(   ) Playing other games, such as baseball, or marbles,
         skipping the rope and so on
(   ) Daydreaming
(   ) Working around home for your family
(   ) Working for other people
(   ) Doing your homework

—   —   —   —   —   —   —   —   —   —

If you care to, you may sign your name here.

THANK YOU

APPENDIX B

Forms Used with Delinquent Girls in State Training Schools

(1) Questionnaire on pre-institutional motion picture experience submitted to delinquent girls in state training school.[1]

1. Age.   Grade.

2. Race: White.   Colored.

3. Nationality.
   Please answer following questions about your experience with movies before you came here.

4. Did you ever imitate anything from motion pictures?
              Yes.   No.
   Please check all the things on the following list that you have imitated from the movies.
        How to wear clothes, fix your hair, make-up, etc.
        How to act with a man.
        How to kiss, flirt, or make love.
        How to shoplift.
        How to drink and smoke.
        How to act at a party.
        How to gamble.
        How to fix up a home.

5. Did the movies ever make you want to live a gay, fast life?
              Yes.   No.

[1] (Ed. note. Question 7 and 11 of this Questionnaire are somewhat ambiguous in character. The statistical data coming from them are given in the test with a recognition of this ambiguity, and are presented only because the autobiographical material gives a reasonable character to the data.)

6. Did the movies ever make you want to go to wild parties, cabarets, or roadhouses?

     Yes.   No.

7. Did going to wild parties, cabarets, roadhouses, etc., like they do in the movies, ever get you into trouble?

     Yes.   No.

Ever lead to your staying away from school?

     Yes.   No.

Ever lead to your running away from home?

     Yes.   No.

Ever lead you to sexual delinquencies?

     Yes.   No.

8. Did motion pictures ever make you want to have fine clothes, automobile, wealth, servants, etc.?

     Yes.   No.

9. Did the movies ever make you want to make a lot of money easily?

     Yes.   No.

Did the movies suggest to you any of the following ideas of making easy money?

   By getting a job and working.

   By shoplifting.

   By "gold-digging" men.

   By gambling.

   By sexual delinquency with men.

   By living with a man and letting him support you.

10. Did you ever do any of these things to get easy money as the result of seeing movies?

     Yes.   No.

(If so, please check right answer.)

   Getting a job and working.

   Shoplifting.

   "Gold-digging" men.

   Gambling.

   Sexual delinquency with men.

   Living with a man and letting him support you.

11. Did wanting fine clothes, automobiles, luxury, and wealth, as shown in the movies, ever make you run away from home?

     Yes.   No.

12. Did the movies ever make you day-dream?
        Yes.   No.
  What did you day-dream about? (Please check following list.)
    A life of luxury and ease, clothes, autos, servants.
    Gay, fast life—wild parties, cabarets, etc.
    Having a lover and making love like they do in the pictures?
    Being a vampire or "gold-digger."

13. Did the movies ever stir you sexually—arouse your passion?
        Yes.   No.

14. Do you usually feel like having a man make love to you after you see a passionate love picture?
        Yes.   No.

15. Do you let men make love or pet you after seeing passionate love pictures?
        Yes.   No.

16. Have you ever engaged in sexual delinquency with a man after you got sexually excited at a movie?
        Yes.   No.

17. Have you ever stayed away from school to go to the movies?
        Yes.   No.

18. Have you ever had fights with your mother or father because you wanted to go to the movies?
        Yes.   No.

19. Did you ever run away from home after such a fight?
        Yes.   No.

20. Have the movies ever made you want to be real good?
        Yes.   No.
  For how long were you good? (Please check right answer.)
    About a day.
    About a week.
    About a month.
    About a year.
    More than a year.

21. What kinds of movies made you want to be good?
    Crime, gangster pictures or pictures which show the ill-fate of women who go wrong.
    Moral, religious, or sentimental pictures.
    Love pictures.
    Fast life pictures.
    Adventure pictures.

22. Did the movies teach you any of the following lessons?
    To beware of boys and men because all they want from a
    girl is sex.
    Not to take lifts from strangers.
    A wild life does not pay.
    Not to be sexually delinquent because you might have a
    child or get diseased.
    The woman always pays the price for a good time.

23. If so, did you ever forget about any such lessons when you
    were with men?
    Yes.   No.

24. Has the ill-fate of women who go wrong in the movies ever
    kept you from doing anything people think is not right?
    Yes.   No.

(2) Rating sheet and form for brief essay on rôle of motion pictures in delinquent behavior submitted to delinquent girls in
state training school.

1. Please read through the following list and then rank them is
   the order in which you think they explain why you got into
   trouble. That is mark the one you feel is most responsible
   for your being here (1), mark the next most responsible (2),
   and so on.
   (   ) Desire to be popular.
   (   ) Broken home (divorce, separation or death of parents,
          step-parent).
   (   ) Poverty.
   (   ) Desire for clothes, automobiles, etc.
   (   ) Movies (love pictures, wild or fast life, luxury, good
          clothes, automobiles, etc.).
   (   ) Girl friends.
   (   ) Drinking.
   (   ) Men.
   (   ) Lack of parental guidance.
   (   ) Desire for a good time, parties, etc.

2. Please write a page or two telling what you think is responsible
   for your getting into trouble. How important do you think
   the movies were in getting you into trouble?

(3) Questionnaire submitted to delinquent girls in state training school on their institutional motion picture experience.

1. What was your age at your last birthday?

2. Where were you born?
   If you were born outside of the United States at what age did you come to this country?

3. Was your mother born in this country?
   Was your father born in this country?

4. How far did you get in school? Please put circle around the last grade or year of school you finished.

   Grammar School   *High School*   *College*   *Graduate work*

   1 2 3 4 5 6 7 8   1 2 3 4   1 2 3 4   1 2 3

5. Please rank the following in the order in which you think they have influenced your life most. That is mark 1, the one you think has had the most importance in your life, mark 2, the next important, and so on.

   (   ) Newspapers   (   ) Books
   (   ) School   (   ) Home
   (   ) Movies   (   ) Playing by yourself.
   (   ) Playing with boys   (   ) Daydreaming—thinking by
                                        yourself
   (   ) Church   (   ) Playing with other girls.

6. How often did you go to the movies at different ages? Please check right number of times for each age column.

	6 to 12 years old	13 to 17	17 and up
Less than once a week	( )	( )	( )
Once a week	( )	( )	( )
More than once, less than four	( )	( )	( )
More than four times a week	( )	( )	( )

7. Please check the right answer to the following for different ages:

	6 to 12 years old	13 to 17	17 and up
I went to school	( )	( )	( )
I worked regularly	( )	( )	( )
I worked once in a while	( )	( )	( )
I did no work	( )	( )	( )

8: Please check the right answer to the following:
  (   ) Married
  (   ) Single
  (   ) Widowed
  (   ) Divorced
  (   ) Separated

9. How old were you when you first got married?

10. Please answer the following questions as truthfully as you can for yourself *at the present time.* They represent our way of becoming acquainted with you. In front of each question, you will find: Yes   No   ?

   Cross out the right answers for each question. Try to answer by Yes or No, if it is possible. If you are not able to say Yes or No, then cross out the question mark.

Yes No ? Do you get stage fright?
Yes No ? Do you take responsibility for introducing people at a party?
Yes No ? Do you worry too long over humiliating experiences?
Yes No ? Do you often feel lonesome, even when you are with other people?
Yes No ? Do you consider yourself a rather nervous person?
Yes No ?. Are your feelings easily hurt?
Yes No ? Are you sometimes the leader at a social affair?
Yes No ? Do ideas often run through your head so that you cannot sleep?
Yes No ? Are you frequently burdened by a sense of remorse?
Yes No ? Do you worry over possible misfortunes?
Yes No ? Are you usually even-tempered and happy in your outlook on life?
Yes No ? Are you troubled with shyness?
Yes No ? Do you daydream frequently?
Yes No ? Have you ever had spells of dizziness?
Yes No ? Do you get discouraged easily?
Yes No ? Do your interests change quickly?
Yes No ? Is it difficult to move you to tears?
Yes No ? Does it bother you to have people watch you at work even when you do it well?
Yes No ? Can you stand criticism without feeling hurt?
Yes No ? Do you make friends easily and quickly?
Yes No ? Are you troubled with the idea that people are watching you on the street?

Yes	No	?	Does your mind often wander badly so that you lose track of what you are doing?
Yes	No	?	Have you ever been depressed because of low marks in school?
Yes	No	?	Are you touchy on various subjects?
Yes	No	?	Are you often in a state of excitement?
Yes	No	?	Do you frequently feel grouchy?
Yes	No	?	Do you feel at ease and self-confident when you recite in class?
Yes	No	?	Do you often feel just miserable?
Yes	No	?	Does some particular useless thought keep coming into your mind to bother you?
Yes	No	?	Do you hesitate to volunteer in a class recitation?
Yes	No	?	Are you usually in good spirits?
Yes	No	?	Do you often experience periods of loneliness?
Yes	No	?	Do you often feel self-conscious in the presence of superiors?
Yes	No	?	Do you lack self-confidence?
Yes	No	?	Do you find it easy to speak in public?
Yes	No	?	Do you usually feel that you are well-dressed and make a good appearance?
Yes	No	?	Do you feel that you must do a thing over several times before you leave it?
Yes	No	?	If you see an accident are you quick to take an active part in giving help?
Yes	No	?	Are you troubled with feelings of inferiority?
Yes	No	?	Is it easy for you to make up your mind and act on your decision?
Yes	No	?	Do you have ups and downs in mood without apparent cause?
Yes	No	?	Are you in general self-confident about your abilities?

[Reprinted from L. L. Thurstone—Personality Schedule (1930). Used by permission University of Chicago Press.]

11. Please rank the following activities that you have here in the order in which you like them. That is mark the activity listed that you like most 1, the one you like next best 2, and so on.

*Order in which
you like them*

Band concerts
Training for a job
Outdoor athletics
Movies

Indoor games
School work
Radio program
Theatrical performance
Conversation—talk periods
Reading—the library
Chapel service
Shop or outdoor work
You may list any other ac-
tivities you wish.

12. Do the movies you see here make you think? (Please check only one of the following.)
  (　) Very much
  (　) Much
  (　) Some
  (　) Very little
  (　) Never

13. Please check some of the following that the movies make you think about most:
  (　) Home life
  (　) Men—fast life
  (　) Getting a job and working
  (　) Life of adventure and thrills
  (　) Keeping out of trouble
  (　) Making money easy somehow
  (　) Getting married and settling down
  (　) Learning a trade
  (　) Crime does not pay
  (　) How to fool the police
  (　) Getting even with society for your imprisonment
  (　) How to make love
  (　) How to wear clothes, fix your hair, etc.
  (　) Having a real fling when you get out

14. Do the movies you see here tire or bore you? (Check only one of the following.)
  (　) Very much
  (　) Much
  (　) Some
  (　) Very little
  (　) Never
What kinds of movies tire or bore you?

15. Do the movies you see here teach you? (Check only one of the following.)
    (   ) Very much
    (   ) Much
    (   ) Some
    (   ) Very little
    (   ) Nothing

16. Please check three of following which the movies teach you most:
    (   ) Ways of getting money easily
    (   ) How to dress right
    (   ) How to keep out of trouble
    (   ) How to make love to a man—how to flirt, kiss, etc.
    (   ) How to fool the police
    (   ) Crime does not pay
    (   ) How to get a job and work
    (   ) How to fix up a home

17. Do the movies you see here stir you up sexually? (Check only one of the following.)
    (   ) Very much
    (   ) Much
    (   ) Some
    (   ) Very little
    (   ) Never

18. Do the movies you see here make you feel cheerful and contented?
    (   ) Very much
    (   ) Much
    (   ) Some
    (   ) Very little
    (   ) Never
    What kinds of movies make you feel cheerful?

19. Do the movies you see here get you excited? (Check one of following.)
    (   ) Very much
    (   ) Much
    (   ) Some
    (   ) Very little
    (   ) Never

20. Please check three of the following scenes that excite you most:
( ) Religious scenes
( ) Gun play
( ) Passionate love pictures
( ) Punishment of criminals
( ) Scenes of good clothes, automobiles, wealth
( ) Loyalty to a friend
( ) Murder scenes
( ) Scenes of home life
( ) Mystery scenes
( ) Stick-up scenes—new ways of pulling jobs
( ) Fooling the police
( ) Wild parties and cabaret scenes

21. Do the movies you see here make you feel like keeping out of trouble after you get out?
( ) Very much
( ) Much
( ) Some
( ) Very little
( ) Never

22. Please rank the following pictures in the order that you like to see them here. That is, mark the one you like to see best 1, the one you like to see next best 2, and so on.
( ) Wild west pictures
( ) Mild love pictures
( ) Serials
( ) Crime pictures
( ) Passionate love pictures
( ) Mystery pictures
( ) Comedies
( ) News reels
( ) Religious pictures—sad pictures
( ) Airplane or adventure pictures

23. Do the movies you see here make you feel bitter toward society, make you feel like you have not had a square deal?
( ) Very much
( ) Much
( ) Some
( ) Very little
( ) Never
What kinds of movies do this?

24. Please check any of the following that the movies you see here show in a way that you like:

( ) College life
( ) Honest life
( ) Fast life—parties, men
( ) Home life
( ) Fighting
( ) Life of the criminal
( ) Hard work
( ) Life of the idle rich
( ) Married life

25. Please rank the following activities that you have here in the order in which you think they will help you keep out of trouble after you get out. That is, mark the one you think helps you most to go straight 1, mark the one that helps you next most 2, and so on.

Order in which they help you keep out of trouble after you get out

Band concerts
Training for a job
Outdoor athletics
Movies
Indoor games
School work
Radio program
Theatrical performance
Conversation—talk periods
Reading—the library
Chapel service
Shop or outdoor work
You may list any other activities you wish.

(4) Guidance sheet for document on institutional motion picture experience submitted to delinquent girls in state training school.

1. Tell why you like to see movies. What "kick" do you get out of them?

2. Tell what kinds of pictures you like to see here. Why do you like to see them? What do you do after you see them? Tell what kinds of pictures you don't like to see. Why don't you like to see them?

3. Tell what the movies you see here make you think about. Do they make you think much? What are the more important things you think about? What kinds of movies make you think most?

4. Tell what the movies you see here teach you. Do they teach you much? What are the more important things you learn from them? What kinds of movies teach you most?

5. Tell what kinds of movies get you excited most. What do you get excited about? What do you do after you see movies that excite you? How do you feel?

6. Describe your feelings when you see movies that show snappy clothes, good automobiles, lots of money. Do such movies make you dissatisfied with your own clothes? Do you wish you had a good car and lots of money? Do such movies make you think about how to make a lot of money? What ways of making money do you think about?

7. Describe your feelings when you see pictures about women that "go wrong." Do you think such pictures are true to life? What ideas do you get from such pictures? Does the kind of life such women lead in the movies make you feel that you would like to be like them? Does the punishment or bad endings some of these women get in the movies make you feel like keeping out of trouble after you get out? Please explain.

8. Do any of the movies you see here make you think of getting married? What kinds of movies do this? Do you get any ideas from the movies of the kind of husband you would like to have? What ideas do you get?

9 Tell if the movies you see here make you feel cheerful and contented. How do they make you feel cheerful? What kinds of pictures do this? Are there other things that are more important in making you feel cheerful? What are they?

10. Tell if the movies you see here make you feel bitter toward society, make you feel that you have not had a square deal? Why do they make you feel that way? What kinds of pictures do this?

11. Describe your feelings when you see passionate love pictures here. Do you like to see them? Do they stir you up? What do you do after you see them? Please describe your experiences fully telling if possible the names of the pictures, actors and actresses, how you felt and what you did.

12. Tell if the movies you see here help you in any way to keep out of trouble after you get out. How do they help you do this? What kinds of pictures do this? Are there other things here more important than the movies in helping you keep out of trouble after you get out? What are they?

APPENDIX C

Forms Used with Male Inmates of State Reformatory

(1) Questionnaire on pre-institutional motion picture experience submitted to male inmates of state reformatory.

1. Rank (1 for first, 2 for second, etc.) the following in the order in which you believe them to have influenced your life: Magazines (   ), Books (   ), Motion pictures (   ), Newspapers (   ), Vaudeville or burlesque shows (   ).

2. List in the order of your preference (1 for first, 2 for second, etc.) the following:

Pictures	Age 6–12	Age 12–17	Age 17–
Wild west			
Mild love pictures			
Gangster pictures			
Serials			
Passionate love pictures			
Mystery pictures			

3. Check any of the following which the movies usually present in a fascinating or attractive way:
   (   ) College life   (   ) Fighting
   (   ) Home life   (   ) Life of wealth
   (   ) Life of the criminal (   ) Hard work
   (   ) Honest life   (   ) Free and unrestrained life

4. Do you find the movies usually (indicate by check mark)
   are exciting?
   make you think a lot?
   teach you a little?
   stir you up sexually?
   tire you or bore you?

5. When you see an exciting picture do you want to (indicate by check mark)
   (   ) make love to a girl?
   (   ) go out and have a good time?

(   ) act tough or fight someone?
(   ) do something daring or adventuresome?
(   ) talk to others about what you have just seen?

6. Have the movies ever led you to do daring, adventuresome things?

7. Do you believe that gangster or burglar pictures are likely to lead boys or young men into crime?
Is there any other kind of picture likely to?
What kind?

8. When you see an adventuresome gangster, burglar, or bandit picture do you
(   ) Feel like you want to be a gangster or burglar?
(   ) Imagine yourself being one, doing big and daring things, and fooling the police?
(   ) Plan to hold up someone, or to pull a job?
(   ) Decide that you would like to be a policeman?
(   ) Feel convinced that the risks and dangers of being a gangster are too great?
(   ) Feel that every gangster and burglar ought to be caught and punished?

9. Do you feel that the movies develop the desire for easy money?
Do you believe that they suggest ways of getting money easily?
What ways?

10. Do you think that the movies give one the desire to carry a gun?
To practice stick-ups with them?

11. Do you think that the punishment given to criminals in the movies is likely to stop one from committing crimes?
Do you think that the punishment given to criminals in the movies is true to life?

12. Has such punishment as shown in the movies ever made you hesitate about carrying out a job?
(If so, name picture and experience.)

13. Have you seen any movies which incited you to commit a crime?
(If so, give picture, and mention what you did.)

14. Have you seen any movies which made you want to be real good, or to go straight?
(If so, give pictures and tell of your experience.)
How long did you want to be good?

15. Have the movies taught you:
    (   ) How to attract girls, how to flirt, kiss, or to make
            love?
    (   ) Ways of stealing?
    (   ) How to fool the police?
    (   ) How to act tough, or act like a big guy?
16. In what ways do you feel that the movies have contributed
    to your own difficulty?

(2) Guidance sheet for document on pre-institutional motion
picture experience submitted to male inmates of state reformatory.

1. Tell as far as you can how the movies influenced your childhood games (such as "Cops and robbers") and whether such
   games made you want to get into the racket. Tell how you
   felt toward the good guy and the bad guy in the pictures you
   saw. As a child, did you ever want to be the bad guy? Did you
   like to take the part of the bad guy in your games?

2. Write about any experience in which the movies (a) tempted
   you to engage in crime, or (b) caused you to imagine yourself
   being a bold gangster or burglar, or (c) led you to pull a job.
   (Give the name of the picture, or who was in it, what was it
   about, and what you did after you saw it.)

3. Tell about any ideas that you have gotten from the movies
   about easy money, or being a smart guy or a big guy. What
   kind of things do they show in pictures of this sort and how
   do you feel when you see them? Describe anything that such
   ideas have had to do with your career.

4. Tell anything that you have learned from the movies about
   crime or ways of committing crime. (Ways of stealing, of
   pulling a job, of fooling the police, opening a safe, and so forth.)
   Have you copied or tried to copy any of these ways? Explain.

5. When you see an exciting and adventuresome picture, do you
   feel brave, tough, or adventuresome? Do you feel like going
   out and doing something daring? Explain how such pictures
   have affected you and what you did after seeing them. (Give
   names of pictures, if you can.)

6. Tell about any experiences in which the movies made you
   hesitate about pulling a job, or made you want to be good and
   go straight. (Give name of the pictures, if you can, and mention briefly what they were about. Tell fully about your experience with them.)

7. Describe briefly how you feel when you see a gangster or burglar picture. Do you think much about whether the picture is true to life? How do you feel about the punishment which the criminal gets in the picture? Explain.

8. Describe the sort of things which the movies ought not to show to be sure that boys won't get ideas of crime from them.

9. Describe your experiences with love and sex pictures. Have you learned from the movies any ways of attracting girls, of flirting, kissing, and making love? Explain. Do you like passionate love pictures? Are you stirred up by them? Have you had any parties after you have seen such pictures? Describe your experiences along this line as fully as you can, naming pictures and actors if you can, and telling what you did.

(3) Questionnaire on institutional motion picture experience submitted to male inmates of state reformatory (Form A, sample of 40).

1. What was your age at your last birthday?
2. Where were you born?
   If you were born outside of the United States at what age did you come to this country?
3. Was your mother born in this country?   Was your father born in this country?
4. How far did you get in school? Please put circle around the last grade or year of school you finished.

Grammar School	High School	College	Graduate work
1 2 3 4 5 6 7 8	1 2 3 4	1 2 3 4	1 2 3

5. Please rank the following in the order in which you think they have influenced your life most. That is mark 1, the one you think has had the most importance in your life, mark 2, the next important, and so on.

( ) Newspapers   ( ) Books
( ) School   ( ) Home
( ) Movies   ( ) Playing by yourself
( ) Playing with the gang   ( ) Daydreaming—think-
( ) Church   ing by yourself

6. How often did you go to the movies at different ages? Please check right number of times for each age column.

	6 to 12 years old	12 to 17	17 and up
Less than once a week	( )	( )	( )
Once a week	( )	( )	( )

More than once, less than
four   ( )   ( )   ( )
More than four times a
week   ( )   ( )   ( )

7. Please check the right answer to the following for different ages:

	6 to 12 years old	12 to 17	17 and up
I went to school	( )	( )	( )
I worked regularly	( )	( )	( )
I worked once in a while	( )	( )	( )
I did no work	( )	( )	( )

8. Please check the right answer to the following:
    ( ) Married
    ( ) Single
    ( ) Widowed
    ( ) Divorced
    ( ) Separated

9. How old were you when you first got married?

10. Please answer the following questions as truthfully as you can
    for yourself *at the present time.* They represent our way of
    becoming acquainted with you. In front of each question, you
    will find: Yes   No   ?
       Cross out the right answers for each question. Try to answer
    by Yes or No, if it is possible. If you are not able to say Yes or
    No, then cross out the question mark.

Yes   No   ?   Do you get stage fright?
Yes   No   ?   Do you take responsibility for introducing people
               at a party?
Yes   No   ?   Do you worry too long over humiliating experiences?
Yes   No   ?   Do you often feel lonesome, even when you are with
               other people?
Yes   No   ?   Do you consider yourself a rather nervous person?
Yes   No   ?   Are your feelings easily hurt?
Yes   No   ?   Are you sometimes the leader at a social affair?
Yes   No   ?   Do ideas often run through your head so that you
               cannot sleep?
Yes   No   ?   Are you frequently burdened by a sense of remorse?
Yes   No   ?   Do you worry over possible misfortunes?
Yes   No   ?   Are you usually even-tempered and happy in your
               outlook on life?
Yes   No   ?   Are you troubled with shyness?
Yes   No   ?   Do you daydream frequently?

Yes	No	?	Have you ever had spells of dizziness?
Yes	No	?	Do you get discouraged easily?
Yes	No	?	Do your interests change quickly?
Yes	No	?	Is it difficult to move you to tears?
Yes	No	?	Does it bother you to have people watch you at work even when you do it well?
Yes	No	?	Can you stand criticism without feeling hurt?
Yes	No	?	Do you make friends easily and quickly?
Yes	No	?	Are you troubled with the idea that people are watching you on the street?
Yes	No	?	Does your mind often wander badly so that you lose track of what you are doing?
Yes	No	?	Have you ever been depressed because of low marks in school?
Yes	No	?	Are you touchy on various subjects?
Yes	No	?	Are you often in a state of excitement?
Yes	No	?	Do you frequently feel grouchy?
Yes	No	?	Do you feel at ease and self-confident when you recite in class?
Yes	No	?	Do you often feel just miserable?
Yes	No	?	Does some particular useless thought keep coming into your mind to bother you?
Yes	No	?	Do you hesitate to volunteer in a class recitation?
Yes	No	?	Are you usually in good spirits?
Yes	No	?	Do you often experience periods of loneliness?
Yes	No	?	Do you often feel self-conscious in the presence of superiors?
Yes	No	?	Do you lack self-confidence?
Yes	No	?	Do you find it easy to speak in public?
Yes	No	?	Do you usually feel that you are well-dressed and make a good appearance?
Yes	No	?	Do you feel that you must do a thing over several times before you leave it?
Yes	No	?	If you see an accident are you quick to take an active part in giving help?
Yes	No	?	Are you troubled with feelings of inferiority?
Yes	No	?	Is it easy for you to make up your mind and act on your decision?
Yes	No	?	Do you have ups and downs in mood without apparent cause?
Yes	No	?	Are you in general self-confident about your abilities?

[Reprinted from L. L. Thurstone—Personality Schedule (1930). Used by permission University of Chicago Press.]

11. Please rank the following activities that you have here in the order in which you like them. That is mark the activity listed that you like most 1, the one you like next best 2, and so on.

*Order in which
you like them*

Band concerts
Training for a job
Outdoor athletics
Movies
Indoor games
School work
Radio program
Theatrical performance
Treatment of prison guards
Conversation—talk periods
Reading—the library
Chapel service
Shop or outdoor work
You may list any other activities you wish.

12. Do the movies you see here make you think? (Please check only one of the following.)
(   ) Very much
(   ) Much
(   ) Some
(   ) Very little
(   ) Never

13. Please check three of the following that the movies make you think about most:
(   ) Home life
(   ) Women—fast life
(   ) Getting a job and working
(   ) Life of adventure and thrills
(   ) Pulling more jobs when you get out
(   ) Going straight
(   ) Making money easy somehow
(   ) Learning a trade
(   ) Crime does not pay
(   ) How to fool the police
(   ) New ways of pulling a job
(   ) Getting even with society for your imprisonment.

14. Do the movies you see here tire or bore you? (Check only one of the following.)

( ) Very much
( ) Much
( ) Some
( ) Very little
( ) Never

What kinds of movies tire or bore you?

15. Do the movies you see here teach you? (Check only one of following.)

( ) Very much
( ) Much
( ) Some
( ) Very little
( ) Nothing

16. Please check three of following which the movies teach you most:

( ) Ways of getting money easily
( ) How to dress right
( ) Ways of pulling jobs
( ) How to go straight
( ) How to make love to a woman—how to flirt, kiss, etc.
( ) How to fool the police
( ) Crime does not pay
( ) New rackets
( ) How to get a job and work
( ) How to fix up a home

17. Do the movies you see here stir you up sexually? (Check only one of the following.)

( ) Very much
( ) Much
( ) Some
( ) Very little
( ) Never

18. Do the movies you see here make you feel cheerful and contented?

( ) Very much
( ) Much
( ) Some
( ) Very little
( ) Never

What kinds of movies make you feel cheerful?

19. Do the movies you see here get you excited? (Check one of following.)
    (   ) Very much
    (   ) Much
    (   ) Some
    (   ) Very little
    (   ) Never

20. Please check three of the following scenes that excite you most:
    (   ) Religious scenes
    (   ) Gun play
    (   ) Passionate love pictures
    (   ) Punishment of criminals
    (   ) Scenes of good clothes, automobiles, wealth
    (   ) Loyalty to a friend
    (   ) Murder scenes
    (   ) Scenes of home life
    (   ) Mystery scenes
    (   ) Stick-up scenes—new ways of pulling jobs
    (   ) Fooling the police

21. Do the movies you see here make you feel like going straight?
    (   ) Very much
    (   ) Much
    (   ) Some
    (   ) Very little
    (   ) Never

22. Please rank the following pictures in the order that you like to see them here. That is, mark the one you like to see best 1, the one you like to see next best 2, and so on.
    (   ) Wild west pictures
    (   ) Mild love pictures
    (   ) Serials
    (   ) Crime pictures
    (   ) Passionate love pictures
    (   ) Mystery pictures
    (   ) Comedies
    (   ) News reels
    (   ) Religious pictures—sad pictures
    (   ) Airplane or adventure pictures

23. Do the movies you see here make you feel bitter toward society, make you feel like you have not had a square deal?
    (   ) Very much
    (   ) Much

(   ) Some
(   ) Very little
(   ) Never
What kinds of movies do this?

24. Please check any of the following that the movies you see here show in a way that you like:

(   ) College life
(   ) Honest life
(   ) Fast life—parties, women
(   ) Home life
(   ) Fighting
(   ) Life of the criminal
(   ) Hard work
(   ) Life of the idle rich

25. Please rank the following activities that you have here in the order in which you think they will help you go straight after you get out. That is, mark the one you think helps you most to go straight 1, mark the one that helps you next most 2, and so on.

*Order in which they
help you go straight*

Band concerts
Training for a job
Outdoor athletics
Movies
Indoor games
School work
Radio program
Theatrical performance
Treatment of prison guards
Conversation—talk periods
Reading—the library
Chapel service
Shop or outdoor work
You may list any other activities you wish.

(4) Guidance sheet for document on institutional motion picture experience submitted to male inmates of state reformatory.

1. Tell why you like to see movies. What "kick" do you get out of them?

2. Tell what kinds of pictures you like to see here. Why do you like to see them? What do you do after you see them? Tell what kinds of pictures you don't like to see. Why don't you like to see them?

3. Tell what the movies you see here make you think about. Do they make you think much? What are the more important things you think about? What kinds of movies make you think most?

4. Tell what the movies you see here teach you. Do they teach you much? What are the more important things you learn from them? What kinds of movies teach you most?

5. Tell what kinds of movies get you excited most. What do you get excited about? What do you do after you see movies that excite you? How do you feel?

6. Describe your feelings when you see movies that show snappy clothes, good automobiles, lots of money. Do such movies make you dissatisfied with your own clothes? Do you wish you had a good car and lots of money? Do such movies make you think about how to make a lot of money? What ways of making money do you think about?

7. Describe your feelings when you see crime pictures. Do you think such pictures are true to life? Do they give you new ideas on how to pull jobs and fool the police? Does the punishment given to criminals in such movies help keep you from pulling another job?

8. Tell if the movies you see here help you in any way to go straight after you get out. How do they help you go straight? What kinds of pictures do this? Are there other things here more important than the movies in helping you go straight? What are they?

9. Tell if the movies you see here make you feel cheerful and contented. How do they make you feel cheerful? What kinds of pictures do this? Are there other things that are more important in making you feel cheerful? What are they?

10. Tell if the movies you see here make you feel bitter toward society, make you feel that you have not had a square deal? Why do they make you feel that way? What kinds of pictures do this?

11. Describe your feelings when you see passionate love pictures here. Do you like to see them? Do they stir you up? What do you do after you see them? Please describe your experiences fully telling if possible the names of the pictures, actors, and actresses, how you felt and what you did.

APPENDIX D

Forms Used with Heads of Institutions

(1) Questionnaire submitted to heads of penal and correctional institutions where motion pictures are not shown.

1. Are there any reasons why motion pictures are not shown in your institution at the present time?   Please explain.

2. Would you show movies if you could?
   To all of your charges?   If not, to which ones of them?

3. Have motion pictures been shown in your institution in the past?   If so, why were they discontinued?

4. Do you think that if movies were shown in your institution it would help to maintain discipline and morale?
   Please give any reasons you may have for your answer.

5. Do you think that if movies are shown at your institution it would help in training and character building?
   Please give any reasons you may have for your answer.

6. Have you had any opportunity to observe the effects of movies on residents of other institutions?

7. Do you feel that the ordinary run of movies shown to boys and youths and girls and young women are likely to lead some of them into lives of delinquency and crime?   Please explain.

(2) Questionnaire submitted to heads of penal and correctional institutions where motion pictures are shown.

1. How often were movies shown in your institution during the last four weeks?   Are they shown more frequently during some seasons such as winter than during others?   Please explain.

2. Do you prohibit attendance at movies for infraction of regulations?
   Do you show movies more often to some groups than others?   How are these groups classified and how often do they see the movies?
   Do you find that prohibiting attendance to movies for breaking regulations helps as a disciplinary measure?
   Please explain.

3. Do you get your films free?   If free, due to whose courtesy?
Do you rent your films?   How do you get your
funds for showing movies?

4. Who selects the pictures you show?
As far as you know is there any set of principles followed in
choosing these pictures?
What are they?
Do you experience any difficulty in obtaining the type of pic-
tures you want?   Please explain.

5. Would you show movies more frequently if you could?
Why?

6. Please give titles of last ten pictures exhibited.

7. What kinds of movies do you think it unwise to show in your
institution?

8. Do you censor the pictures you show?   What
kinds of scenes do you cut out if any?
Who does the censoring?   Is it necessary
to do much censoring?

9. How much do you think the movies shown help in maintaining
discipline and morale?   (Please check opposite appropriate
effect.)
     Distinctly favorable for maintaining discipline and morale
     Mainly favorable for maintaining discipline and morale
     Sometimes favorable for maintaining discipline and morale
     Of no noticeable effect for maintaining discipline and morale
     Sometimes unfavorable for maintaining discipline and
     morale
     Mainly unfavorable for maintaining discipline and morale
     Distinctly unfavorable for maintaining discipline and
     morale

10. Please explain as fully as possible if you wish, the reason for
the answer you have given.

11. How much do you think the movies help in training and
character building?
     Distinctly favorable for training and character building
     Mainly favorable for training and character building
     Sometimes favorable for training and character building
     Of no noticeable effect for training and character building
     Sometimes unfavorable for training and character building
     Mainly unfavorable for training and character building
     Distinctly unfavorable for training and character building

12. Please explain as fully as possible, if you wish, the reasons for the answer you have given.

13. Could you please quote verbatim, as nearly as possible, typical statements of your charges about the pictures?
What have you observed are the more important effects of the pictures on your charges?

14. Do you know of any cases which have been led by the pictures shown in your institution to give up lives of delinquency?
If so, about how many?
Please explain as much as possible the details of each case, such as, the nature of the delinquency, time spent in institution by him, the nature of the pictures seen by him, and why you believe the movies to be the cause of his reformation?

15. Do you know of any cases upon whom the pictures shown in the institution have had a harmful effect?   If so, about how many?
Please explain as fully as possible the details of each case, such as the nature of the delinquency, time spent in institution by him, the nature of the pictures seen by him, and why you believe the movies to have been harmful.

16. Please give the names of any pictures that you feel have had a noticeably harmful effect on your charges.
If possible please explain why.

17. Please give the names of any pictures that you feel have had a noticeably good effect on your charges.
If possible, please explain why.

18. Rank those of the following activities given in your institution in the order of their importance in maintaining discipline and morale (1 for most important, 2 for next important, etc.)

Chapel services	Radio program
Band concerts	Theatrical performance
Outdoor athletics	Reading
Indoor games	Shop or outdoor work
Movies	Other activities, specify.
School work	

19. Rank those of the following activities given in your institution in the order of their importance in training and character building, (1 for most important, 2 for next important, etc.)
Chapel services
Band concerts

Outdoor athletics
Vocational training
Indoor games
Movies
School work
Radio program
Theatrical performance
Reading—library
Shop or outdoor work

20. Have motion pictures ever been discontinued in your institution in the past? Please explain.

21. Do you feel that the ordinary run of movies shown to boys and youths and girls and young women are likely to lead any of them into a life of delinquency and crime? Please explain why.